Frontispiece – Maria Colwell

REMEMBER MARIA

by

JOHN G. HOWELLS

M.D., F.R.C. Psych., D.P.M.
*Director, The Institute of
Family Psychiatry, Ipswich,
England*

BUTTERWORTHS

ENGLAND: BUTTERWORTH & CO. (PUBLISHERS) LTD.
                  LONDON: 88 Kingsway, WC2B 6AB

AUSTRALIA: BUTTERWORTHS (PTY.) LTD
                  SYDNEY: 586 Pacific Highway, 2067
                  MELBOURNE: 343 Little Collins Street, 3000
                  BRISBANE: 240 Queen Street, 4000

CANADA: BUTTERWORTH & CO. (CANADA) LTD.
                  TORONTO: 14 Curity Avenue, 374

NEW ZEALAND: BUTTERWORTHS OF NEW ZEALAND LTD.
                  WELLINGTON: 26–28 Waring Taylor Street, 1

SOUTH AFRICA: BUTTERWORTH & CO. (SOUTH AFRICA) (PTY.) LTD.
                  DURBAN: 152–154 Gale Street

Suggested U.D.C. Number: 362·74/·75

ISBN 0 407 38541 X

Printed by R. J. Acford Ltd, Industrial Estate, Chichester, Sussex

Contents

Preface

Maria Colwell was killed by misconceptions about the care of children.

Maria Colwell was battered to death by her stepfather while she was in his and her natural mother's care. She had been taken from her foster parents, after having been in their care for six years, and had been returned to her natural mother.

Maria Colwell was killed by ignorance, not by ill intention. Her case is one of many. It behoves us to wait no longer before examining our basic ideas of child care. This is the purpose of this book. True knowledge will lead to the right practices. The point of this book is not to attack any individuals, organizations or professions. Its aim is to reveal the misconceptions that lie behind dangerous and destructive practices.

Some readers may feel that the conclusions reached here are obvious. They would be right, yet those conclusions still need description. Maria's neighbours called for help for her. They did not subscribe to the misconceptions that led to her death. They knew three things: (1) They — sensible, kindly, mature fathers and mothers — knew, not from books, but from experience of life, that the natural home is not always the best place for the child, for sometimes the parent–child relationship is damaging rather than helpful. (2) They knew that Maria could have been cared for better by her foster parents than by her natural parents; they understood that the bond between a child and a caring adult depends on the quality of the care and not on the degree of biological relatedness. (3) They knew that Maria, in her exceptional circumstances, needed to be separated from her natural mother; she needed to be rescued. They understood because they were parents with strong bonds with their own children, they knew what a strong bond means, and could tell when none existed.

More children than ever before are battered, and some to death, in the United Kingdom. More children than ever before are at risk. The very services created to help them add to the risk. In medicine we term this situation an iatrogenic condition, i.e. an illness caused by the treatment itself. For instance, because of misconceptions based on a lack of knowledge, for centuries we bled people for all and every illness. A few benefited from it, many were killed by it. Misconceptions are rife in our service to help children. The care of our children is in the hands of a national service, which has become almost a monopoly. Issues often handled by the public with experience, spontaneous feeling and common sense have not yet been thought out within this service.

Sadly, very sadly, because of the misconceptions to be outlined in this book, children at risk in their own homes are seldom rescued. The whole machine set up by our goodwill to care for our children has served to increase the danger to them, because of wrong notions. Our service unwittingly supports damaging forces by binding children to the natural family whatever the circumstances. Hence the child has been placed in a defenceless position − his parents have all the rights. He must take whatever punishment they mete out, emotional and physical, to the point of death.

A family home is not normally a dangerous place. For as long as we have recorded history, there is testimony that it is the safest and best environment for the child. But we now know that sometimes, exceptionally, the home can be dangerous and hurtful. In these unusual circumstances special measures must be taken to protect the child to whom we cannot deny the same right to safety that we grant to adults.

Maria's case was special and demanded unusual measures, but she was dealt with as if she was in normal circumstances. That this happened was not due to ill intention. We, the public − and the services that we create, control and pay for − intend that all our children should experience a happy life. Our services did not kill Maria by ill intention, they failed because they subscribe to wrong concepts. Misconceptions led to the wrong practices that killed Maria Colwell.

These same misconceptions place at risk a large number of children all over the world. People are properly concerned when children, orphaned and in the custody of child care authorities, are badly handled, but overlook the fact − for it is less obvious − that many more children are at risk of great emotional damage in their own homes. About 1 child in 200 lives outside his family and some of these children are at risk, but 199 children out of 200 live with their own families. They too can be at risk — and in far greater numbers.

Maria was one of many children who meet death at the hands of their natural parents. Many more are injured and physically hurt. But hidden is a far greater peril. Physical hurt is easy to detect. Emotional hurt is difficult to detect. Many, many more children are emotionally hurt than are physically hurt. Battered children are only the tip of the iceberg of child distress.

Good care in childhood is at the core of our well-being. Our families make or break us. This is why we feel so strongly, and rightly so, about children. We are the product of our childhood — it makes us what we are, joyful or miserable adults. The stakes are high. Perhaps we have not recognized how high they are. For every child killed like Maria, there are 50 in misery, less obvious, but still in misery. And childhood misery becomes the misery of adults.

For 20 years the author has attempted through the scientific press to correct misconceptions in child care. A book devoted to the subject and written for the child care expert has been in preparation for some time, but now it has been put aside in favour of an address to those who often seem to understand better, the informed public. However, the fact that experts are sometimes wrong is no argument for not having experts. The best engineers can act on wrong concepts; in consequence bridges can fall into rivers, but we still need engineers — and good bridges.

The examination of Maria's brief tragic life is an unavoidable, if painful, starting point for a number of questions about our notions on the care of children. These questions are the main part of this book. It is not the purpose of this book to enquire into matters of administration or organization in Maria's case. The Court of Inquiry is well equipped to do this. However, right concepts can lead to right practice and the pages that follow will attempt to point to these. It is important to ventilate all points of view, work down to basic concepts, and arrive, quickly, at sounder practices. While we talk children suffer. They cry and are not heard. We must talk, but not for too long.

The Institute of Family Psychiatry,   *John G. Howells*
Ipswich, England

Chapter 1

The Tragedy of Maria Colwell

Maria's case is taken as an example of many emotionally deprived children because it offers an opportunity for considering some basic issues in child care. Thus it is necessary to give only the essential facts, which help us to focus on the issues of concern to us.

Maria's life can be divided into three periods. The first was a brief spell, of about six months, with her natural father and mother, Mr. and Mrs. Colwell; she was removed from them because of her mother's neglect.

The second period, of about six years, and the happiest, was spent with her father's sister and her husband, Mr. and Mrs Cooper.

The third period, of about one year three months, was spent with her natural mother and her mother's second husband, the child's stepfather — Mr. and Mrs. Kepple. This unhappy period ended in her death at the hands of her stepfather, Mr. Kepple. We shall need to give more detailed consideration to the third period.

Maria was born in the spring of 1965. Her father left her mother shortly after her birth. Thus she lived with the two parents together for a very short time. About four months after her birth, Maria's father, aged 28, died as the result of heart trouble and therefore passed out of her life. By October 1965, about six months after her birth, there was concern about the care of Maria and her three older siblings by the natural mother. An inspector of the National Society for the Prevention of Cruelty to Children (NSPCC) investigated the neglect of the children. Maria, the youngest of the children and still an infant, was placed in the care of her aunt, Mrs. Cooper. For a brief period she went back to her mother, but when the NSPCC obtained a court order giving parental rights to the East Sussex County Council she was returned to Mrs. Cooper.

Maria remained with Mr. and Mrs. Cooper for six years, until she was about six and a half years old. During evidence to the Court of Inquiry Mrs. Cooper referred to Maria as 'my baby', and a baby she was when Mrs. Cooper first began mothering her. No complaint was made of her care during this time. She was regarded as happily brought up and the Coopers wished to adopt her. Thus of the six and a half years of Maria's early life about six months was a period of neglect and six years a period of normal care.

Towards the end of Maria's care by the Coopers, there occurred a number of events which ended in Maria returning to the care of her natural mother. Mrs. Colwell had in the meantime moved about a great deal; indeed it was said that she had nineteen different addresses in four and a half years. However, by July 1970 Mrs. Colwell set up home with Mr. Kepple, and after Maria's return, became Mrs. Kepple in May 1973. She had three children by Mr. Kepple and these lived with them. Mrs. Kepple has had ten children by four men — a child before she married Mr. Colwell, a number of children by Mr. Colwell, a number of children by Mr. Kepple and, following Mr. Kepple's recent imprisonment, a child by a fourth man.

Quarrels developed between Mrs. Kepple and her first husband's sister, Mrs. Cooper, over Mrs. Kepple's access to Maria. By June 1971 the tension between the competing mothers was such that it was said to affect Maria's health. A doctor diagnosed Maria as being depressed. The tension is one possible explanation of her depression. But there is another much more likely and more direct explanation. Tension between two people does not hurt a third as much as a directly harmful situation between that third person and another. Thus Maria's symptoms may have resulted from the trauma of direct contact with her mother; it was claimed by the Coopers that the child spent time with her natural mother with great reluctance. If Maria was hurt by contact with her mother and feared that her mother would acquire her, looked at from Maria's standpoint rather than that of her natural mother, there was reason for Maria's fright and alarm — if not of dread. Evidence from anyone, including a child, can be wrong and biased. But all should be heard, and given the weight due in the circumstances. A child's opinion, however, is rarely as explicit as that of an adult and usually carries less authority, but nevertheless it should be heard.

We can only guess at Maria's distress. The account of her feelings is not available to us. We do not know whether she had an opportunity to

Figure 1 – Mrs Pauline Kepple, mother of Maria Colwell

express it or whether anyone sought it. She was not at the court hearing. We do know, however, the testimony of others caught in similar circumstances. Two instances will be quoted here.

In 1970 a mother sought the return of her two daughters who had been looked after by a foster mother for three years (*Daily Express*, 13 July 1970). The natural mother and the foster mother agreed to a 'love test', i.e. the natural mother visited the foster mother's house to discover which of them the children wanted. The test was soon discontinued. The natural mother said, 'It is clear they were happy and well loved. The last thing I want is to see the children "upset". It would only be right to let the J.'s adopt the children.' The foster mother commented, 'It was a terrible situation with the two girls sobbing themselves to sleep at night because no-one could assure them they would not have to leave'.

An adult recounts, in an admirably clear fashion (*The Times*, 22 July 1970), what a child can feel:

When I was seven years old the woman who ran the home and who stood as foster-mother to me married and kept me with her and her husband with another child who had spent her whole life there.

From when I can remember, until my mother went off to Canada when I was 12 at the beginning of the war with her sons leaving me behind, my mother persistently told me each time I saw her that she would be having me to live with her, but in the event her nerve would fail and nothing would happen. Each time the suggestion came up I felt as if the whole world that I knew was disintegrating and the thought of leaving my beloved foster-mother for a stranger was a continuing anguish.

When my real mother returned from Canada at the end of the War I was over 16 and could choose not to live with her. It is impossible to describe the strain which the uncertainty of such a situation imposes on children. They are completely powerless to influence events which shape their lives and it seems to the child that it is the victim of utterly irrational and damaging actions.

I always knew what the situation was – I never supposed my foster-mother to be my real mother – but there was no question in my mind that I not only wanted but desperately needed to stay where I had lived all my life and received the affection and care on which children so deeply depend.

The argument that blood is thicker than water is completely invalid to me; I never felt the slightest affinity with my mother in spite of the blood tie; on the contrary I felt the deepest commitment to my foster-mother who to me was the only real parent that I had.

In Maria's case the supervisory authority decided to return her to her mother for a trial period – this in October 1971. In November 1971, the risk of moving a child from a known benevolent situation to an untried one of possible hazard, a longer trial period would normally have been thought prudent, indeed essential. After all, the local authority, and not the Coopers, had parental rights and thus if they feared any interference by the Coopers it could have been controlled by them. It was known that the natural mother had not given exemplary care to her children. If Mr. Kepple's parenting capacity was not known, then this lack of knowledge argued for caution. The counsel for the mother, at the Inquiry, described Mr. Kepple as 'a violent and belligerent man who drank a lot, was work shy and had a bad temper' (*The Times*, 8 December 1973). Surely, a close contact with the family for a few occasions, one hour at a time, would have brought out Mr. Kepple's characteristics before Maria was ever returned to the family. If the task became complex, as indeed sometimes it does, referral could have been made to the psychiatric services.

For Maria to return to the care of her mother it was necessary, of course, to revoke the Court Order which six years before had given parental rights to the local authority. This necessitated the natural mother and stepfather stating to a court their case for the return of parental rights. The local authority had to decide whether or not to support the Kepples' case. Their grounds for doing so we will discuss in a moment. The court revoked the Order, but wisely retained a Supervision Order. This is least allowed the local authority the right to visit and supervise. It meant, however, that the local authority, having lost parental rights, would have to return to a court to re-obtain them.

The court may have thoroughly gone into the matter, but it seems that scant attention was given to any view that the foster parents (who had cared for Maria for six of her six and a half years) might have held, for they were not invited to the hearing and, it is said, did not know of it. The hearing was attended only by the natural mother and the officers of the local authority, who supported the natural mother. The court did not seek an independent opinion, such as they could have obtained from a child psychiatrist. These events raise the question whether foster parenting is considered as weighty a matter as natural parenting. Should Maria have been removed from her natural parents after six years in their care, would their views not have been canvassed? Here the choice lay between a natural mother and stepfather, Mr. and Mrs. Kepple, and an aunt and uncle, Mr. and Mrs. Cooper. Had the Kepples been found to be as adequate as the Coopers, it would still seem reasonable to have left Maria in the care of the Coopers, as their parenting was known to be successful — a policy of leaving well alone. In fact there were strong doubts about the adequacy of the Kepples. Should both homes have been unsatisfactory, the local authority had after what appears to have been a very brief period of trial, Maria went back permanently into the care of her natural mother. Bearing in mind the duty and the power, if the child's interest was the paramount consideration, to place Maria in another and happier foster home.

This moment in time was critical for Maria. Whoever is involved in such a decision carries responsibility that makes or breaks a life. It cannot be said that such decisions are taken lightly in the United Kingdom. Often, those who decide rely upon or are guided by established viewpoints or opinions, or principles. Wise opinions lead to happy conclusions; unwise opinions to the reverse. Thus we must examine with care the reasons for the decisions in Maria's case and the principles on which they were based. I quote from the account given in *The Daily Telegraph*, 6 November 1973:

... any decision about Maria's future would involve stress and trauma for her. In a report which she made at the time, she said 'on balance it was felt that future plans should be directed towards her eventual return to her mother. While she remained with the Coopers she would continue to be the centre of conflict.'

It is unlikely that the Coopers would be able to deal well with her feelings in adolescence concerning her natural parents and it is possible that at this age she would herself decide to return to her mother.

The witness said that a child had a 'special feeling' about her natural parents, whether or not that parent was on the scene at the time. She felt it highly desirable that the child should have as much contact as possible with her natural parents.

The major and overwhelmingly decisive factor that led to the removal of Maria from the foster parents was the supposed 'special feeling' about her natural parents (although one was dead) and thus the need to be with her mother. Here the child care authorities leant on established opinion – the supposed ever present strong bond between child and mother. It is one of the main objects of this book to show that this bond is not ever present. They leant also on another viewpoint – that the mother–child bond is unique. Another main object of this book is to display that this bond is also present between children and fathers, aunts, uncles, foster parents, adoptive parents, teachers and all those who can love children; in some circumstances it can be equal to and even outweigh the mother–child bond. These misconceptions inevitably lead to another that can be drastic and deadly in its consequences – children should not be removed from their mother whatever the circumstances – and its corollary – children should be returned to their natural parents whenever the opportunity. Thus Maria had to leave her foster parents in favour of her natural mother and thereafter could not be separated from her.

Figure 2 – William Kepple, stepfather of the dead girl Maria Colwell

The overriding factor in the decision to take Maria from her foster parents was that she was cut off from *natural mothering*. Indeed one teacher stated in evidence (*The Daily Telegraph*, 17 October 1973) that a social worker had told her that the child was 'too emotionally involved with her auntie'. But adequate fostering of a child must include emotional involvement, otherwise the child is in a cold environment.

Another factor based on misconceptions about natural parenting turns around the tension between the natural mother and the foster mother. Whether Maria stayed with the Coopers or moved to the Kepples, it seemed to the local authority officers, was likely to lead to 'stress and tension'. With the Coopers she was the centre of conflict between them and the Kepples. It might be argued that, as the local authority had parental rights, the tension could have been controlled. Indeed, if it was in Maria's interest, the parenting by the Coopers could have been given greater weight that the parenting by the Kepples — even to the point of reducing or abolishing visits by Maria to her natural mother and stepfather. To restrict visiting by the Kepples would have called for a careful assessment of the natural mother and stepfather and of their relationship with Maria.

A local authority spokesman commented in this connection (*The Times*, 24 November 1973), 'There was no real likelihood of deflecting her from pursuing her objective', i.e. Mrs. Kepple obtaining Maria. Another spokesman (*Evening Standard*, 8 November 1973) said, 'But we felt Mrs. Kepple would never give up her pressure for access.' It would seem that the whole point of our child care procedures is being forgotten. The procedures are for the benefit of the child and not for that of the child care authorities. They are meant to be a buffer that protects the child. The authorities should take the weight of pressure and not the child. If adequate, they should contend with the situation and do what is right for the child.

Another factor bearing on the same element, natural mothering, but based on misconception, made the Coopers a risk in the eyes of the authorities, in as much as they might not, indeed were 'unlikely', to have dealt with Maria's feelings towards her natural parents in her adolescence. The author has no direct knowledge of the Coopers and on what evidence this judgement was made. If their care of her in her childhood was adequate, there were grounds for expecting that it would be equally adequate in her adolescence. To think otherwise was pure conjecture and it was unwise to base action not on the realities of the moment but on speculations, of doubtful weight, in the future.

The authorities felt that the hazards in the two homes were equal and one witness (*The Times*, 21 November 1973) made explicit the one, and apparently only one, objection to the Coopers as foster parents: 'Maria was not allowed to have feelings in her own right, feelings that would have made possible a transfer of roots. They blocked efforts to help Maria in this respect.' Essentially, then, the objection was that the foster parents did not inculcate in Maria the notion that the natural parent is more important than any other parent whatever the circumstances. But probably the Coopers, like most of us, did not subscribe to this view. They particularly did not believe in it in the situation in which Maria found herself; and they were sadly proved right. They loved the child, as parents should, after parenting her for six years and had reasonable prospects of adopting her; many would have said that adoption should have given Maria permanent roots long before her sixth birthday. This criticism of the Coopers seems completely outweighed by their evident and proven capacity to parent the child and Maria's evident flourishing in their care. It is impossible to accept that the risk with the Coopers was as great as with the Kepples. If it was truly the same, she should have remained where she was, as has been said before.

The views held by fostered or adopted children about their natural parents is worth further comment here. In my clinical experience, children, and indeed most people, are more concerned with reality than with phantasy, with real people more than with phantoms. It is a hangover from outmoded views of the psyche to imagine that we are hurt by phantasies. We are hurt by ever present reality and we use phantasy as a compensation. It is my experience that happy fostered and adopted children show little interest in their natural parents other than that of normal curiosity; the reality of good parenting by foster and adoptive parents is enough. They do not show an inclination to abandon foster and adoptive parents in adolescence. This typical attitude of a secure foster child can be seen in the letter quoted on page 4. The position is quite different in the case of unhappy foster and adopted children. Here it is to be expected that in their unhappiness they argue to themselves that things would have been happier if they were with their natural parents; they form an image of the desirable which sadly often does not coincide with reality. On the rare occurrences when it is achieved, a confrontation with the natural parents may lead to disillusionment and further unhappiness, or to joy, depending on the quality of the natural parents. Unhappy foster and adoptive children are a minority, but of course are the majority of those seen by the caring professions; happiness does not call for help. It may be this selection factor which had led to excessive weight being given to the view that fostered or adopted adolescents have a strong pull back to the natural parent.

It is of the utmost importance to realize that if a foster or adoptive child is unhappy, it is not because of the break in the bond with the natural parent. They are unhappy because of disturbing events in the present — usually within the foster or adoptive homes. To give the child news of his natural parents will not change these present events. The disturbing events in the present can be changed only by changing the present. Returning the child to the natural parents if they have the capacity for right caring, the wish to have the child with them and are able to do so, may be one procedure. Sometimes the natural parents are suitable, but their circumstances make it impossible for them to take the child. In the great majority of instances the disturbing and unhappy events that led the child to be parted from his natural parents still operate, and a meeting, even if agreed by the natural parents, may lead to disillusionment and further trauma for the child. Maria's case illustrates how the previous disturbing events of her infancy were still in operation six years later.

Continuing our explanation of the reasons that prompted the return of Maria to her natural mother, it is necessary to quote one witness from the local authority (*The Times*, 24 November 1973) who said that 'her department would never have agreed to the return had they had any suspicion that the child would be at physical risk'. But surely judgements should not turn around physical risk alone. Children can, and Maria did, suffer from emotional trauma. The physical damage is the obvious damage; it usually coexists with emotional damage. Even in the absence of physical damage there may be emotional damage sufficient to wreck a child as a person, as a potential marriage partner and as a potential parent. The choice between two homes turns around a global assessment of which home will best provide all these ingredients of emotional and physical care likely to produce a healthy happy adult with a capacity to provide the same ingredients in turn for his own children.

It is also necessary to point out the misjudgements that can accrue from overemphasis on maternal care and giving too little or no weight to paternal care. Mr. Kepple was as significant a parental figure, even if negative, as Mrs. Kepple. Indeed it was he who killed Maria.

The above misconceptions, whatever the contributing factors, killed Maria Colwell.

Maria's life, after her return to the natural mother, her stepfather and half-siblings was a chapter of misery. Misfortune grew on misfortune. The tale is too sad to relate in detail. Maria's own tale is only available in frightened fragments. None were able, though many were willing, to stand by her side in her ordeal, for her parents had all the rights. She was a citizen without rights. No adult, even captive in time of war, is without rights. It is an objective of this book to denounce such injustice. What makes us, supposedly lovers of children, stand exclusively on the side of parents? We must digress a moment to consider this curious phenomenon. Natural parents rise in protest at the welfare of children not being given paramount importance. Presumably, with a capacity for the loving care of children, parents feel for children. However, in the caring professions often the reverse is true. Parental rights are given the greatest weight. Wrong theory is mostly responsible for this attitude, and for its uncritical acceptance by training establishments. Or is it a wish to rid society of responsibility by making parenting completely a matter for parents? But there may be deeper reasons. Is frustrated parenting expressing itself? Or is there sometimes an idealization of parents arising from a deprived childhood? If the former reasons are true, the matter is quickly put right by correct theory and teaching. If the latter is the explanation, it speaks for more careful selection of personnel for the helping professions.

Maria passed into the care of the Kepples in October 1971. When this happened her foster parents for six years lost their rights too. Although the natural mother had access to Maria when in the care of her aunt and uncle, the reverse did not happen. But foster parents also have feelings. We trade on their good feelings when we wish them to care for children. Is it fair to ignore them when it is convenient? But this is in conformity with the wrong principle that foster parenting is less worthy than natural parenting. This case also raises the question for how long foster parents have to give loving care to children before they can adopt them.

Maria was in an uncongenial climate. Her plight, however, did not go unnoticed. In the last nine months of her life, 30 complaints were made by 17 people or groups of people about the way she was cared for by her natural mother and stepfather. The complaints referred to loss of weight, neglect, injuries, scape-goating, and excessive physical demands made on Maria. Complaints were made to the NSPCC, the local authority, the housing authority and the police. The complaints were largely made by neighbours — mothers and fathers of the locality. Their actions led to investigations. Routine supervision and investigation led to 56 visits to the home by a number of people. At various times Maria was seen by social workers, education welfare officers, teachers, doctors, and NSPCC inspectors. Some contemplated action. Indeed, some action was taken, but none of it was decisive. Maria was frequently absent from school despite 17 calls by the education welfare officer. Her absence denied her a school health examination that might have led to action. From 18 November to her death in January 1973, she was never at school.

In October 1972 the foster mother, Mrs. Cooper, asked to see Maria, but her request was not granted. In November, as the result of a complaint, the parents were warned by the police not to leave the children alone in the evenings. An attempt to get Maria to a school doctor in early December failed as the parents did not keep the appointment, and this failure went unnoticed. Her general practitioner was satisfied with her condition in early December. The social worker in immediate supervision had been unable to see her for five and a half months prior to 1 August, but visits recommenced in early December. Though the child's disturbed state must have been conspicuous, no-one in the medical, social or educational fields thought fit to get psychiatric help for her and her family.

One myth is exploded here. To change complex long-standing fixed family structures is a lengthy, expert and difficult task. To expect family visitors to adjust families in a few visits is crying for the moon. Even 56 visits did not, and could not, have changed the essential emotional state of the Kepple family. The time available in the field is far better spent on assessment. Plans can then be realistic. To know early on that Maria should not be returned to the Kepples not only would have saved Maria, but also a considerable expenditure of resources. Correct assessments, with expert help if required, often lead to the deployment of the community's help to protect the child and ameliorate its circumstances, even if a change of family is not possible. In some instances — Maria's was one of these — separation procedures are essential.

The complaints about the care of Maria came from outside the home. One witness at the Court of Inquiry did, however, have access to the house — this was Sandra, Maria's 18 year old aunt. She returned to the Court of Inquiry to correct the evidence she had previously given in which she had denied any ill-treatment of Maria. Her account (*The Sun*, 28 November 1973) was not accepted by Mrs. Kepple.

It was a few weeks before Christmas. Kepple was at work and his wife, Pauline, was going to a nearby phone box to take a call from him. Sandra went on:

'Maria was the only child who was in bed. The others were up and dressed to go to the phone box with Pauline. Pauline said she could not take Maria with her because if she did, the child would run off. I asked her if I could go up and see Maria. When I got to her bedroom, there was no handle on the door and I could not open it. Pauline said she had to take it out because if she did not, Maria would run off. She opened the door for me with the handle while I went in to see Maria. The room was dark. I asked Maria how she was. She did not answer. She just lay there. She was frightened. She seemed as if she wanted to tell me something but she wouldn't. I kissed her goodnight. When I left, Pauline removed the door handle again.'

On another occasion, Sandra was babysitting while the Kepples went out. Before they left, Kepple and Sandra were alone with Maria. Sandra told the inquiry:

'He told Maria to go to bed. I had already told her she could stay up and watch telly because she did not have to go to school the next morning. She looked at me as if she wanted to know what to do. He told her to go up again but she wouldn't. He slapped Maria across the face. It was a double slap, with the front of his hand and then the back. I went mad. I said he shouldn't pick on a little girl and he should find someone older. There was no reason to hit her. Then he went for Maria again. I picked up a vase and threw it at him. I pushed her out of the way behind me. He started shouting. We had an argument about Maria. He started swearing at me. He said he had lost his temper. After Kepple hit Maria, she had a graze on her face on the right cheek. It was all red. He must have caught her with his nails.'

Then Sandra told how Mrs. Kepple bought sweets for her children. She got a chocolate bar and a nougat bar for all except Maria. Sandra added that Mrs. Kepple said: 'She doesn't want any.' Then Maria's grandmother, Mrs. Lillian Tester, bought her sweets. But Maria said she would not eat them until she got home.

On the way, Sandra continued, one of the Kepple daughters, Teresa, continually kicked the back of Maria's legs. 'Mrs. Tester told Pauline to give Teresa a smack. But Teresa had said: "She won't hit me because I'll tell my dad." Teresa was spoiled. Kepple treated her like a pet, as if she was the only one there.'

On the evening of 6 January Mr. and Mrs. Kepple returned home from the pub. Maria was watching television. It seems that the stepfather, intoxicated and angry, thought that she objected to being told to go to bed. He beat her savagely. Next morning the parents wheeled her in the pram to hospital. She was found to be dead. Her injuries included brain damage, two black eyes, extensive bruising of the face, back, buttocks, arms and legs, internal injuries and an empty stomach. The post-mortem examination also revealed a right rib fractured on a previous occasion. Her weight at age seven was 36 lb, only two thirds of what it should have been.

Chapter 2

The Issues

From the account of Maria Colwell's case arises a need to ask many questions. Many are matters of administration, of organization and of law. Questions can be asked as to whether the supervision of the natural home was adequate, whether the supervision of staff was adequate and wise, whether less staff would have been more effective, whether co-ordination of agencies was what it should be, whether misevaluations were made, and whether there was indecision and inefficiency. These questions are best answered by the Court of Inquiry, which is able to assess and weigh the evidence at first hand.

While not denying the importance of the above matters they are not as important as the basic misconceptions that led to the decision which in turn led to the sorry chapter of events. **These misconceptions killed Maria Colwell – and they kill many other children.**

Three basic, but linked, issues are selected for discussion in the next three chapters.

THE FIRST BASIC ISSUE

Overriding weight was given to the 'special feeling' between child and mother; it was assumed to be ever present. Chapter 3 is concerned with the nature of *The Mystical Bond* between parent and child.

THE SECOND BASIC ISSUE

It is implied, by the overriding weight given to the mother–child bond, that any other loving bond must in all circumstances be less important.

Indeed the mother–child bond is said to be unique; like no other. For instance, throughout the account of Maria Colwell's case it is clear that foster parenting was given less weight than natural parenting. Thus a chapter is devoted to the nature of *Loving Care.*

THE THIRD BASIC ISSUE

The above views held in conjunction lead to the idea that a child's natural family is better for him than any other family. Thus separation of child from the natural parents is regarded as the greatest evil in all circumstances. This is a cruel doctrine. Carried to its rigid extreme, as it was in Maria Colwell's case, there is no escape for the child, however misused. Thus a chapter is devoted to *The Evil of No-Separation.* From this it emerges how the mistake of confusing separation with deprivation has been at the root of wrong action. Its inevitable consequence, once accepted by the child care organizations, was that children were actually encouraged to stay in or return to damaging homes, whatever the circumstances or consequences. Thus more children are battered, and many suffer from the less obvious but still damaging consequences of emotional deprivation; emotional trauma is no less severe in its effects than physical trauma.

EXTRA ISSUES

Three extra issues arise from Maria's case and the plight of all emotionally deprived children.

The question can be asked, 'what leads to the inability of parents to nurture their children?' The unfolding of this issue can only result in compassion. Parents were once children; their childhood experience is passed on in their actions towards their own children and in this way emotional illness passes down the generations. Disturbed families lead to disturbed families, hence a chapter on *The Vicious Spiral.*

It is possible to intervene in this vicious spiral and the means of intervention deserve a brief review in the chapter *The Quest for Health.*

Lastly, it is only fitting to discuss how the correction of the misconceptions can immediately lead to adjustments in child care procedures, hence a chapter entitled *Towards the Right Care.*

Chapter 3

The Mystical Bond

INTRODUCTION

A bond, a link, a liking, an empathy, a pulling towards one another, can exist between any two people or groups of people. Indeed, also between a person and an animal.

The link between natural parent and child is assumed by some experts to be especially strong. Furthermore it is said to be everpresent and of such value to the child that it must be regarded as essential to his welfare, so irreplaceable that it outweighs all other relationships. It is said to be a biological tie, and the term 'blood tie', is often employed. Even when child and parent are separated at birth, it is said that it is so powerful that it attracts the two together after a passage of years, even when the child has become adolescent. Indeed the only objection to the Coopers as parents in the view of the local authority officers was the supposed inability of the Coopers to prepare Maria for a return to her natural mother, for whom she would be craving as an adolescent.

Although the expression 'bond with natural parent' is employed, in practice this is frequently interpreted as meaning bond with natural mother rather than with natural father — this was the interpretation in Maria's case, the link had to be maintained with her natural mother even if it involved fathering by a non-natural father and parting from a natural aunt.

Presumably, a link between two people must have a mutual value for it to be maintained. In the case of the parent—child relationship it must

17

provide gratification for the parent and protection and care for the child. If it continues to adolescence, it must bring more than care and protection for the adolescent, as he is past the need for them; possibly there is some gratification available to the adolescent which is not present within any other bonding. One of the issues here is whose gratification is the more important — that of the parent or that of the child?

Notions about this bonding of parent and child are often so vague, ill defined, and so difficult to demonstrate that it can truly be called mysterious or mystical. The view is taken here that it is not mystical, but essentially of the same nature as any linkage between two people.

Even if the concept is vague it is still strongly held. In Maria's case this was the factor that truly determined her return to her natural mother. This 'special feeling' existed, it was maintained; 'it always exists in children and parents'. Its dictates, it is held, had to be satisfied and this outweighed all other considerations, such as the bond that had existed between Maria and her foster parents for six years. The natural bond was believed to be of more value than that with foster parents or others, despite the fact that it had not protected Maria from neglect before her separation from the mother as an infant. It did not protect her from neglect, pain and death following her return to the mother. It was argued that to miss this link would cause Maria to suffer in some way, even though she had a loving bond with her foster parents, and that in adolescence Maria would so hunger for the link that she would seek it out and maybe even abandon her foster parents. This idea was upheld despite powerful evidence that the child strongly resisted the return to her mother; indeed it is clear that the pressure put on her to restore this link and break the bond with the persons she regarded as parents was responsible for a sharp deterioration in Maria's wellbeing even before she left the foster parents. She had to be dragged by force from her foster parents.

This misconception about the mother–child bond is strongly held and denies the evident pain that it sometimes causes to the child. It is reminiscent of the Inquisition, where the greatest pain, indignity, degredation, violence, misuse of justice and death were still justified by a wrongfully held belief.

We must re-examine this 'special feeling', this mystical bond of parent and child, before it does more terrible harm. In Maria's case, it must be stated, not everyone accepted the power of this natural bond; a teacher much concerned about Maria's welfare was quoted as saying (*The Daily Telegraph*, 12 October, 1973), 'I don't think she ever accepted Mrs. Kepple as her mother.' Perhaps most of the public would have echoed her belief.

The Times (6 August, 1966) reported a public protest at a situation not dissimilar to that of Maria's. A High Court Judge ruled that a girl who had been in the care of the foster parents for 6 years should be returned to her natural mother. The child refused to leave the foster parents' home. A petition signed by 700 people in the County of Buckinghamshire, where the foster parents lived, was sent to the Home Secretary protesting at the child being taken from them. A similar petition was organized in the Oxfordshire village where the natural mother lived. The viewpoint of the public was well expressed in a quotation by one of the sponsors of the petition, 'Any mother will understand what we are trying to do. This girl has been with her foster parents for six years. They are the only parents she has ever known. She calls them "Mummy" and "Daddy". The real mother is a complete stranger to her.' The feelings of natural parents who know a true bond between parent and child is favourable to children. They love and care for children and realize that attainment of this love and care is paramount. If, in a particular case, it can be done best by foster parents they support them. This was not a protest by foster parents for the rights of foster parents. This was a protest by natural parents, who knowing and understanding children's need of love and care, wished to promote the interest of the child.

Many examples could be given of how the notion of a blood tie, the mystical bond, influences decisions about the care of children. One clear-cut example will suffice. Here the matter was to fought out in the Court of Appeal and 'the mystical bond' won the day. The case can be summarized as follows.

A man wished to marry a young woman and a child was deliberately conceived. The mother decided not to marry the man and indeed tried to conceal the child's birth from the father. The child was born in July 1964, and, without father's knowledge, the child was handed over to potential adopters in August. The child was in the care of the potential adopters for 18 months. The father went to court to seek the return of the child to himself, the natural father. The Judge decided that the child should be handed over to the natural father. The potential adopters appealed and the case was heard in the Court of Appeal. With the presiding Judge dissenting, the court agreed to support the decision of the previous Judge in handing the child over to his natural father.

The point of major interest to us here is the grounds on which the judgement was made. The presiding Judge held that the welfare of the child was paramount and could be best served by leaving the child with the potential adopters, who had taken care of him from the age of one month. The two other Lord Justices held that the tie of blood was of overriding importance. One of the two latter Lord Justices expressed the view that there was 'an instinctive tie between parent and child' and he maintained that the child in this case 'would lose an important factor in the development of his personality if he were not brought up by his natural parent.'

This view makes clear at least part of the reason for the misconception. It can be proved without question that a child may inherit certain physical traits from his parents, e.g. colour of eyes, height, brain capacity, and thus it is assumed that he must also inherit emotional characteristics. The latter is difficult to demonstrate and there is ample evidence that many emotional characteristics are produced by direct communication in childhood between the child and those nearest to him. However, should it be accepted that some emotional characteristics are inherited, it is logical to assume that these are not necessarily to the child's advantage. In the physical sphere a child can inherit many handicaps from his parents which may be of great disadvantage to him, e.g. some forms of paralysis and of blindness. Furthermore, any inherited emotional characteristics might be capable of modification by the emotional environment in which the child lives – either in exaggerating or attenuating these characteristics.

If the emotional bond between parent and child is inherited (and there is room for serious doubt) it appears at times to take a form which is to the disadvantage of the child's personality and upbringing and could lead to his destruction. The bond can at times be less than benevolent, indeed downright cruel. It should also be said that even if parental characteristics are inherited by the child before birth, it does not seem possible that he can inherit any more after birth. Indeed if the inherited characteristics are to his disadvantage, it would argue for his upbringing in a new milieu capable of improving them.

Some authorities have made an analogy between the mystical parent–child bond and the 'imprinting' of ducklings on the mother duck. Making deductions about human behaviour from the behaviour of animals calls for caution and this particular analogy is facile. As a demonstration of an adaptive mechanism in a duck it is fascinating and important. If one wished to draw conclusions from the 'imprinting' mechanism of ducklings, one could draw quite opposing conclusions from those stated above. The ducklings can be made to 'imprint' on man and adopt him as a parent figure. Thus we could argue that this instinctive bond is a very flexible and capricious mechanism and is especially geared to making foster parenting an easy matter.

THE CRUEL BONDS

It might be supposed that every parent loves his child. But history records many accounts of parents having malevolent tendencies towards their children. There is space for a few examples only here.

In mythology we have the instance of Medea who cut her children's throats. The study of primitive cultures shows that infanticide was widely practiced, e.g. some Australian Aboriginal mothers liked 'baby meat' and regarded it as a delicacy.

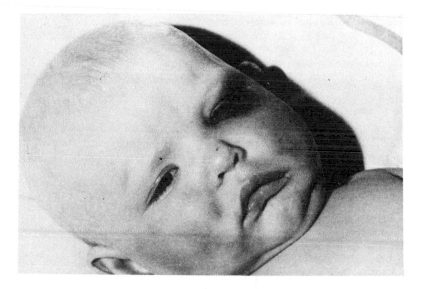

Figure 3 — Shocking injuries were inflicted by the father of this baby girl who disturbed his sleep when she cried in the night. Her left eye was almost closed from the brutal assault and her body extensively bruised

Samuel Johnson, in his *Lives of the Poets,* has many profound things to say about the relationship between the poet Savage and his mother. He could see that hate and homicidal inclinations by the mother had entered into this relationship. Savage's mother wished him hung and gave evidence against him at Bath Assizes. He was aquitted. This was Johnson's commentary:

This was perhaps the first time that ever she discovered a sense of shame, and on this occasion the power of wit was very conspicuous; the wretch who had, without scruple, proclaimed herself an adultress, and who had first endeavoured to starve her son, then to transport him, and afterwards to hang him, was not able to bear the representation of her own conduct, but fled from reproach, though she felt no pain from guilt, and left Bath with the utmost haste, to shelter herself among the crowds of London.

The sensitive Johnson understood also that while the mother's attacks could destroy Savage, there was also a less obvious damage inflicted on the son; to live with such a mother is a gross deprivation that leads to permanent incapacities. Dr. Johnson goes on:

> This mother is still alive, and may perhaps even yet, though malice was so often defeated, enjoy the pleasure of reflecting, that the life, which she often endeavoured to destroy, was shortened by her maternal offices; that though she could not transport her son to the plantations, put him in the shop of a mechanic, or hasten the hand of the public executioner, she has yet had the satisfaction of embittering all his hours, and forcing him into exigencies that hurried on his death.

Johnson clearly understood the damage of emotional trauma.

From our own files at the Institute of Family Psychiatry comes an extract from a letter of a woman to her mother-in-law, who was caring for the woman's child during the week. Who would change places with this child? The mother's legal right over this girl, her unwanted child, overrides the rights of the child. She wrote:

> When I read your letter I got so vexed that if you were living a little nearer I would come down the same day and throw a heavy lashing on Susan's hide . . . I will be coming up just like the devil after her, only that I won't have his horns . . . when you speak to her and she stretches out her mouth give her a little bit of food for the week just for her not to die and do not give her any cover at nights, and do not light the heater for her to get warmth. Just drag her out of the bed in the early mornings. Nothing more to say. Hoping to see you this weekend.

Is the natural parenting here benevolent? Would the proponents of the natural bond hypothesis wish to keep this child with this mother?

Many children who are born are of course often not desired by their parents. Professor Baird compared over a ten-year period in Aberdeen the actual number of children born with the number of desired children. The number of children born was 30 per cent more than the desired number. Of 226 women, 53 had 76 unwanted children. Many of these children, undesired before birth, are accepted subsequently, but such children are at a much higher risk of non-acceptance than desired children. Some will never be accepted by either the mother or father and sometimes by neither parent.

The 'special feeling' between parent and child does not prevent some parents from battering their children. Today approximatelyy 1 in 20 homicides in the USA are directed towards children. The figures take no account of the children killed in pregnancy by induced abortion. It is somewhat higher in the United Kingdom. Resnick, in *Modern Perspectives in Psycho-Obstetrics* (1972), reviews the reasons for child destruction found in history: population control, illegitimacy, inability to look after the child, greed for power or money, superstition, congenital defects, and ritual sacrifice. Under Roman law fathers had a right to kill their children. Among Mohare Indians, half-breeds were killed at birth. The killing of female infants was common in many cultures.

In nearly all infanticides, the mother is the killer. In murders involving children in the first 24 hours after their birth the mother is invariably the murderer. Though the mother appears to be the most common child murderer, it does not mean that she is necessarily more hostile than the father; she may have stronger motivations as well as more opportunities for the act.

The 'special feeling' between parent and child does not prevent parents from killing their children, nor does it prevent them from harming them. Since Caffey's report, in 1946, of multiple fractures caused to children by abuse, increasing attention has been given to what was termed by Kempe 'the battered child syndrome'. Most victims are under four years of age and many under two years. It cannot be over-emphasized that this is not a syndrome of battering by strangers or foster parents, this is a syndrome involving natural parents, a situation where the 'special feeling' has failed. About 4,600 cases a year occur in the United Kingdom. Six children per 1,000 live births is another estimate. It is also not easy to estimate the increase in the number of children involved. The late Professor Camps, Chairman of a Home Office Committee on Battered Babies, told a meeting of the Royal Medico-Psychological Association in November 1969, that it was a recent development and an acute increase was occurring. Mr. John Cronin, asking a question in the House of Commons in 1970, stated that the NSPCC was receiving notifications of 35–40 new cases each month, which represented a fourfold increase on previous figures. Of the 4,600 battered children it is estimated that about 700 children die each year. This amounts to about two deaths a day in the United Kingdom.

Whether or not there is an increase in the battered child syndrome it is clear that despite the attention given to it in the last ten years there has been no decline. Major obstacles to rescuing the children and adding greatly to the risk are the misconceptions described here. Maria Colwell's case was a classic example of the battered child syndrome and the failure of the 'special feeling' between parent and child. While her case was under investigation, four other cases out of many were described in a *Sunday Times* article (11 November, 1973):

Samantha Ralph. Nine months old. Battered to death by stepfather after being discharged by mistake only four hours after her admission to Worcester Royal Infirmary as suspected 'battered baby'. Consultant who released her had not seen her admission papers, on which another doctor had written 'Query — battered baby'. Samantha then had fractured arm, bruising and tooth ripped out. On same night was beaten to death. Stepfather also murdered Samantha's brother and sister; now serving life sentence for murder. Behind-closed-doors inquiry by Birmingham regional hospital board will consider how Samantha was released from the infirmary. Inquiry ordered by Sir Keith Joseph, Health and Social Services Secretary. Some hospital doctors want the inquiry to be held in public.

Peter Taylor. Aged two years. Starved to death while strapped in his pram at his home in Hipswell, North Riding, June 1972. Alsation dog lying under kitchen table had been dead three weeks. Peter's mother separated from her husband, had seven other children — three illegitimate — living with relatives. On probation for theft but no probation officer had gained entry to her home since March that year. They had no right of entry. Some months before Peter died, police broke into house, fed starving dog. Welfare officer knew nothing of incident. The mother, Dorothy Taylor, aged 36, sentenced to four years for manslaughter. North Riding social services held private inquiry. A spokesman said the report 'more or less exonerated everybody.'

The Daily Telegraph (17 October, 1972) reported on the same child:

The mother admitted a charge of the manslaughter of her son Peter. Mr. John Johnson, prosecuting, said that although she had been staying in a house only 10 minutes away, she did not return home for a week, by which time the child was dead. Mr. Johnson said that she had shown utter disregard for the child's welfare. Peter had died from malnutrition while strapped in his pram which was upholstered with flock and had no mattress. Pieces of flock were found scattered about the pram, and Mr. Johnson said one shuddered to think of the child scrabbling with his little hands in the pram.

Graham Bagnall. Aged two years. Died five weeks after returning from foster parents' home to the home of his mother and stepfather at Madeley, Shropshire. Graham was returned at mother's request in April 1972. Stepfather, Benjamin Smith, had history of violence; he had once strangled five pigs. Pathologist found Graham's hair had been wrenched from head and right arm pulled out of socket. Twice before death, Graham's injuries, including a fractured leg, had been brought to attention of the welfare authorities. Mother, Eileen Smith, 22, serving two years for manslaughter; husband committed to Rampton. Shropshire social services department inquiry cleared social workers engaged on case of any careless or reckless professional judgement, but criticized communications failures.

Child X. A boy aged 14 months (name withheld for legal reasons) died three days after being discharged from a hospital due to a misunderstanding by a doctor, who believed he was acting under instructions. Ten days before, family doctor had admitted boy to hospital. At the inquest, boy's injuries were listed as: ruptured liver, fracture of skull and both thighs, other injuries in various parts of body. Inquest

Figure 4 – A moment of heartbreak for a frightened and bewildered little girl and her distressed foster mother. This nine-year-old girl had been cared for by her foster mother since she was a young baby and was finally reclaimed by her natural mother who had six other children, all of whom had been in care

was adjourned pending the outcome of a murder trial. But the coroner said that with the exception of two doctors, no one considered reporting the case to the social services department or the NSPCC for a decision on whether the boy should be placed in care. An inquiry will be held, but it will be held behind closed doors.

In one matter the battered child is fortunate. There are evident signs of trauma on his body that attract the attention of others and which can be demonstrated at a court hearing. However, more children are physically hurt, sometimes continually over a long period of time, but never to the point when the damage is visible. Other neglected and deprived children receive no physical abuse for they are abused verbally and by adverse attitudes and behaviour; no damage is visible other than chronic misery for those who can discern it. Yet another group are not positively misused at all; they are merely ignored and the minimum care given to keep up appearances. The battered child is the tip of the iceberg of deprivation of the right care. This point will be taken up again later for it has great importance for the services designed to help children. The system of care must cater for all these children. Only a small minority are battered children.

Not only can the relationship of mother to child be a hostile one, but so can be the relationship of child to mother. Such a case was reported in *The Daily Telegraph*, 26 October, 1973. A boy of 12 told of whacking with a cane by his mother. He got up at 6.30 a.m., made tea for his parents, practised on the piano for 30 minutes and did homework before breakfast. On his way to school his mother tested him on the previous day's homework. One day his mother rebuked his brother for playing the piano. This seems to have been the last straw. He killed his mother. He said, 'I wanted to hurt Mummy because I was annoyed with her' and 'I ran my fingers along the knife and thought how sharp it was. I stabbed her.'

Earlier I recalled Dr. Samuel Johnson's commentary on the hostility shown by his mother to the poet Savage. It was reciprocated by the son who took his revenge in his poem, *The Bastard*. Johnson comments:

He now thought himself again at liberty to expose the cruelty of his mother, and therefore, I believe, about this time, published *The Bastard*, a poem remarkable for the vivacious sallies of thought in the beginning, where he makes a pompous enumeration of the imaginary advantages of basic birth; and the pathetick sentiments at the end, where he recounts the real calamities which he suffered by the crime of his parents.

Hostility, of course, may not only be directed by a child to the mother, it can be towards the father. In passing judgement on a divorce case (*The Daily Telegraph*, 3 November, 1973) the Judge commented that 'Fear reigned even though this was a father who meant well for his children and thought he was doing his duty.' The father would 'belt them when they were little . . . He beat the boys with a leather belt an eighth of an inch thick.' One child said there were 'good hidings by the score.' Parents reap as they sow. One son in the witness box said, 'I hate my father. He is the worst man I have ever met. I hate him for what he did to me.'

The above instances question the idea that loving care is an inevitable, inherent part of parenting. Parental feeling can sometimes be a damaging, destroying, lethal force. To produce a balance it is necessary to emphasize the *sometimes.* Most frequently parenting is a joyful, merry, rewarding, immensely satisfying experience for parent and child. But it is a denial of facts to assume that it is always so. It is an unpleasant truth, but in any service for children we must face the facts as they are.

THE ROOTS OF LOVING

The potential ability to love is given to all of us. Whether it develops or not is determined by our experiences as children. Those who have been loved develop the ability to love. Those who have experienced emotional warmth can express it. Those who have been nurtured on the milk of human kindness are kind. As for the source of the inability to love, Shakespeare has this to say 'Love, loving not itself, none other can' (*Richard II,* V, iii, 87).

Usually a child is loved by his whole family. From conception he is the child of joyful parents, and, if he is not the first child, his brothers and sisters will also be looking forward to his arrival. The womb is not entirely a place of safety. He may suffer the physical hazards of german measles in his mother, of drugs taken by his mother, of incompatability of his blood with hers, etc. There is also reason to believe that he may suffer emotional hazard while still in the womb. It seems that agitated mothers tend to produce babies of lighter weight. Some midwives assert that some children are more temperamental at birth. Shakespeare certainly believed that intrauterine influences could do damage to a child's body and mind. We need not be reluctant to consult opinion from the past as we do not seem to have made much progress today with our views of child care.

In Shakespeare's play the character Gloucester, later Richard III, had no doubt that his deformity was caused by lack of love from his mother even before birth — 'love forswore me.' A newborn bear is licked into shape by the dam, but to him was denied the love that even animals have as a birthright and he felt like an 'unlicked bear whelp.'

> ". . . , love forswore me in my mother's womb;
> And, for I should not deal in her soft laws,

She did corrupt frail nature with some bribe
To shrink mine arm up like a wither'd shrub;
To make an envious mountain on my back,
Where sits deformity to mock my body;
To shape my legs of an unequal size;
To disproportion me in every part,
Like to a chaos, or an unlick'd bear-whelp
That carries no impression like the dam."

(Henry VI, Part III, III, ii, 153–162)

At birth the child is left in his family. Here he receives love or hate or both from a number of people: his mother, father, brothers and sisters, grandparents, his nanny and so forth. He is surrounded with love or hate or a mixture of the two. Most children are loved and can love. Some are indifferently loved and love indifferently. A few are hated and hate in turn.

I emphasize that the child is in a group and can be loved by all its members. This fact is of great importance. That nature puts us in a group is no accident. Denied love by one person, we can obtain it from another. Indeed the child left to himself gravitates to those who love him. The chances of two parents being unloving are much less than the chance of one being so. That no-one in a group can express love is even less likely, though it can and does occur.

There is still much to be known about the roots of loving and of the best care of children, hence our immediate predicament. Or perhaps false knowledge blinds us to the obvious lessons of the long history of mankind. For instance, we do not know with certainty how long an unloving experience has to last for it to do permanent damage. Impression, rather than the proof of investigation, suggests that unloving in the early years is most damaging. Impression suggests also that some improvement is possible later. Even in adolescence an unloved youngster can respond to a considerable extent if given concentrated love for two to three years; a long exposure to loving is essential. Love is a force as powerful as hate, but it requires time in which to act. Loving spouses soften unloved partners. Yet they need time, and the older they marry the more difficult it becomes.

Loved children become loving parents, of that there is no doubt. That we should be loved is not genetically determined, nor is it inevitable. It happens to most people and most parents are loving. When it does not occur it has to be faced as a fact. The parent is then handicapped. We remove the handicap if we can. While we love the unloving parent, and that is the only way of helping, we must share compassion with the child and see that he is loved too. The child needs protection

from indifference and hate and the opportunity to have the benefits of
being loved.

HONEST HATERS

Some parents can talk about the hate for one or more of their children.
Many more could, if we made it easy for them.

I recall a mother who came to see me. Her request was simple:
'Please help me give my boy away.' A mature intelligent woman, she told
her story. A happy first marriage with a houseful of happy children. 'I can
prove to you they were happy. They are all married and all have happy
marriages.' Then the husband died. In her loneliness she married a
friend of her husband. 'A disaster', she said. They had nothing in
common, 'I am bad for him, you know. That is why he drinks.' She
escaped into business. A little boy was then born to her. 'I swear to you
that I am a kind person. My older children know. But I can't take to
Johnny. I try hard, but I can't. I don't hurt him, I just don't want to be
with him.' So the child is left with the alcoholic father, and he hurts
him. 'It's not right. We ought not to have him. My husband doesn't
want him.' Her problem was that no-one would believe her. Theory said
that she must be full of warm mothering feelings and therefore the
child should stay. In desperation she even asked a solicitor to examine
the laws of other countries to see if they could help.

A not dissimilar situation involved a little girl who died of malnutrition at 11 months (*The Guardian,* 16 January, 1970). The mother
stated that two months before the baby died she started hitting her
children. She and a social worker discussed the matter with her doctor.
They all agreed that the child should be taken away from the mother
and cared for elsewhere. But higher authority disagreed and felt she
should look after the child herself, because of the likely ill effect of
'parting the child from her mother.' The mother stated 'after that I
looked after Tina as best I could.' The care was inadequate and the
child died. The Coroner commented to the mother 'you are obviously
not capable of looking after your children . . .' He added for the whole
world to hear, 'I can't see the point of leaving a child with its mother
merely to let it die of starvation . . .'

The trouble is that a parent is not allowed to admit to lack of
parental feelings. Theory insists that parents are always so full of warm
feelings towards their children and that they delude themselves if they
deny it.

The reason for citing these two instances is to emphasize the value of
making it easy for parents to discuss their true feelings. But if the finger
of blame is pointed at them, then they never will. Thus we deny parents

the right to co-operate with us in helping the child or children they neglect. Guilt is often at the root of clinging to children. If it is shameful to reveal inability to love one's children, then parents will for ever hide their true feelings. The false doctrine of the ever present 'special feeling' of love between parent and child is at the bottom of our troubles.

If the truth can be tolerated, that as victims of our own circumstances we possess varying capacities for parenting, we are in a more advantageous position. This can be accepted without blame, it need precipitate no guilt and a co-operative effort of parents and helper can lead to the best solution. Naturally, if the parents know that in extreme circumstances their child goes, not to an inferior situation but to one of advantage to the child, to foster parenting as good as natural parenting, then this helps them to accept the parting, temporary or permanent.

CONCLUSION

We are forced to conclude that the parent—child bond is not mystical, nor is it ever present. It is of the same essential nature as any bond between two humans. The capacity to love children is largely the product of a loving experience in childhood and is minimally influenced by special circumstances in the parent. There is a scale of loving in parents — most have great capacity, some have little, a few have none; it is a matter of degree. It is important to assess the situation as it is. Right assessments combined with right attitudes by helpers lead to effective decisions.

Those best fitted to estimate the value of a particular parent—child relationship are those who have enjoyed a good one. They have from their own experience a standard which they can consult. Some of the elemental matters of living cannot be gleaned from books; one must consult experience. This fact accounts for the natural spontaneous expression of feeling by the public from time to time — which we curb at our peril. It tells us also something of the necessary qualities of any worker in the helping professions to whom we entrust our children.

Chapter 4

Loving Care

INTRODUCTION

We know from the foregoing evidence that the parent–child bond is usually present but not everpresent. When present, it varies in degree of strength.

Now we need to ask, is the parent–child bond unique? Can nothing else be a substitute for it? Is it of a different quality from any other bond between child and another person? Is any other bond a second best? In Maria's case we recall the comment of one witness at the Inquiry (*The Times*, 21 November 1973). 'Mrs. Kepple's blood tie with the girl influenced decisions. She could not be regarded in the same light as a potential foster mother.'

My answer is that the mother–child bond is not unique. It is essentially of the same quality as any other relationship between two people. While all relationships are essentially the same, each one has a number of characteristics particular to itself, e.g. a mother loving a child is essentially the same process as the child loving the mother, but they each have their flavours (the mother is older, the child younger, etc.). That a child has the capacity to love more than one person is of immense biological significance – if the child looses one relationship he can flourish on another. The flexibility is his lifeline.

It is as well to recall again that when mention is made of the parent–child relationship it invariably refers to the mother–child relationship. We notice that in Maria's case no reference is made of the Mr. Kepple – Maria relationship. This is common.

To understand where we have gone wrong we have to turn to psychoanalytical theory. From this the notion has grown, despite contrary everyday experience, that a child requires a continuous relationship with one object figure in its early years. That one object is held to be the mother. Indeed, as I shall mention later, fathering is not regarded in psychoanalytical literature as an entity in the first two years of the child's life. Hence the emphasis is put exclusively on the mother–child bond. This is obviously wrong. A child is brought up in a discontinuous relationship with a number of people from birth – mummy hands Willie to daddy while she pours the tea, he shares daddy's biscuit, slips from daddy's knee to play with Margaret on the floor and the puppy comes up and licks off what is left of the biscuit. This is group life – family life. Willie loves them all and they all love him.

So ingrained has become the idea of the exclusive importance of the natural mother, that even loving care by another person, in Maria's case by a foster mother for a period of six years, is regarded as of no importance. Faced by the extremity of this view, analytical writers often qualify it by saying that a child needs a continuous relationship with a mother or a permanent mother substitute. In practice no weight is given to the permanent mother substitute – as we saw with Maria, a few months of care by her natural mother outweighed six years of care by her foster mother. It is far better to say simply that a child needs loving care.

When we make errors in human affairs, they are often seen to be stark, obvious, fundamental – once they are grasped. No more striking example is available than that of intelligent, educated, experienced people accepting for the last 70 years the 'one continuous object' hypothesis while living in their own families in a group life. This is a mass delusion of child care experts, not accepted by the public, but forming the basis of action by authorities.

We must now address ourselves in more detail to the question: is the mother–child bond essentially different from any other and thus of overriding importance in the care of the young? An excursion into the animal kingdom will allow us to see the matter in perspective. The fact that families rather than mothers bring up children is capable of substantial proof and this will follow. That mothering is essentially the same as other relationships will become clear in a consideration of fathering. That loving care can be supplied by a number of people will then be demonstrated. The implications of the flexibility of parenting will then be drawn.

CARING IN THE ANIMAL KINGDOM

Does nature rely on one way only for the caring of the young in the animal kingdom? Indeed, does it rely solely on mother care or even parent care? The answer, as we shall see, is an emphatic No. That the young be brought up is more important in Nature than the method employed. Nature is flexible and diverse in its methods. It seeks the best solution in each particular set of circumstances.

The variety and flexibility of nature can be seen in its methods of reproduction—division, budding, autogamy, conjugation, mutation, copulation and parthenogenesis. Nature will use what meets the requirements of the situation—in summer, green aphids reproduce by parthenogenesis, but male and females pair in the autumn. Some animals, e.g. snails, are hermaphrodite and either fertilize themselves or from one another.

Similarly, the main lesson to be found from the study of the care given to young animals is that nature is flexible. The need is to nurture the young so as to continue the species. Depending on the situation, nature will use a variety of means to achieve its purpose. As will be seen, parenting in many forms will be employed. Most important to the young is not *who* offers the care, but that care is given. The intensity of care and quality of care varies with the species—nature meets the need by means appropriate to the situation with a broad concept of parenting and a flexible utilization of the means available. *Parenting* is more important than the parent.

To demonstrate the great variety of methods that are employed by nature a few examples will be given.

No care by parents

The grayling butterflies, male and female, meet only to mate. The female lays her eggs on objects that will provide food for the caterpillars and thereafter leaves them. Many female fish lay their eggs and then give them no further care. Turtles, frogs and spiders behave similarly. In some species of shell fish and sea urchins, the male and female cells are discharged, meet by chance, and are given no parental care. The worm supplies the protection of a cocoon, but no care.

Equal care by parents

In the herring gull, the parents take turns in sitting on the eggs. The eggs are never left alone. After hatching, each parent will feed the chicks by regurgitation and defend them against predators. In the

Ringed Plover, male and female take turns in looking after the young from the first hatch and the eggs of the second hatch. Hobbies, unlike herring gulls, have a strict division of labour between male and female. The female, who is the larger of the two, stands guard over the young, while the male does the food hunting for the whole family. With foxes, the male at first feeds the female and the young; later both feed the young. Adelie and King penguins share the care of the young.

Switching of roles

In some animals it is possible for a switching of roles to take place. In kestrels, for instance, should the female die, the male will take on her task of feeding the young in addition to his own task of hunting for the food. Again, among partridges, the father spends most of his time on the look out, while the mother cares for the offspring and in moments of great danger conducts them to safety. But if the mother should die, the father takes over the task of protecting the young and finding food for them.

Care mainly by the female

In sheep there is exclusive care of the lambs by the ewe. In some varieties of Cichlid fish, the eggs are hatched and young cared for in the mouth of the female. In kestrels, the male hunts for food and the female protects the young and cares for them. Some female scorpions devour the male after copulation; therefore no male care is possible. Praying mantises also devour the male after copulation.

Multiple mothering

In a pride of lions, the young will be fed by the nearest lioness. Amongst elephants, in order to protect them from tigers, the young are placed between the mother and another female elephant, the 'Aunt', both of whom offer care.

Care by groups

In hamsters and mice not only the parents but anyone handy, e.g. adolescents, single males and females, will look after the young.

Foster parents

The female cuckoo lays her eggs in the nest of another species and the young cuckoo is thereafter cared for by the foster parents. Both in scorpions and tarantulas the female will take the offspring of others and foster them—as noted originally by Fabre. In elephants, the tendency to foster is so well developed that the adult childless female elephants may adopt calves of others, or even human children; they may become greatly attached to a child who may be able to take great liberties with the huge foster parents.

Care by servants

In the honey bee, the male fertilizes the queen, the queen lays the eggs; all other duties are performed by worker bees, infertile females. One of the functions of the worker is the care of the young – to be a nanny. Similar conditions are found in termites.

Care in a crèche

When the young Emperor penguins are of an age when both parents have to search for food, they are cared for in a crèche. Adelie penguins also have these kindergartens.

Care by siblings

In moth mites, the male offspring assist in the birth of the females and then immediately impregnate them – demonstrating sibling care and incest.

Care by father

In the stickleback, the male selects the territory for his nest and builds it. He attracts the female and persuades her to spawn in his nest. The male may receive eggs from a number of females. Their work consists only in supplying the eggs and after that it is completely over. Thereafter the male fertilizes the eggs, cares for them and brings up the young. Caring for the eggs includes guarding them and 'fanning' them by inducing a flow of current over them. The young are kept together in a swarm by the father, who is quick to chase and catch in his mouth the wandering young.

In the case of Emperor penguins, care is predominantly by the male as the young live in the male pouch while the female goes off in search of fish. Darwin's frogs of Chile use the male vocal pouch as a nest where the young are incubated and emerge as young frogs. The female sea-horse lays her eggs in a pouch within the male, who thereafter has the care of the eggs and of the young.

Care of the young in other anthropoids

Especial attention must be given to the primate animals most closely related to man. As in man, diversity of methods of care is the striking finding.

Infant care can be a group activity involving different age groups and both adult sexes. Russell's commentary on hierarchies in Japanese monkey bands states that the females approve of male interest in infants and, when females with young are having their next babies, middle rank male leaders and middle rank sub-leaders may take charge of the one year olds. Baby sitting is a way of ingratiating themselves with the females.

In baboons, the birth of a new infant absorbs the attention of the entire troop. From the moment the birth is discovered, the mother in continuously surrounded by the other baboons, who walk beside her and sit as close as possible when she rests. All the adult males of the troop are sensitive to the slightest distress cries of a young infant and will viciously attack any one who comes between an infant and the troop. By the end of the tenth month the infant, who until now has depended largely upon its mother for both companionship and protection, looks to its peers for companionship and to the adult males for protection.

From the two-month observation of an infant female that had lost its mother, Devore illustrates how close a relationship can become between a female infant and an adult male. The sick infant was the male's constant companion, grooming him through the day, walking in his shadow when the troop moved, and sleeping beside him in the trees at night.

Perhaps the most striking example of exclusive male care is provided by the marmosets of South America, the male takes the young to the female for suckling, but this is the only child care allowed to her.

It appears that in anthropoid primates many varieties of child care are found — whole group, joint male and female, exclusively female, multiple female, kindergarten and exclusively male.

Summary

This brief study of infant care demonstrates the variety of methods employed in the animal kingdom for the care of the young, methods that are repeated in human societies. That care is given, is more important than the method, or the individual employed.

Nature is flexible and takes the situation into account, replacing one method by another, if this is more efficacious in a new situation. In chimpanzees, as clan feeling is not well developed, the young must rely on a strong and sustained maternal interest; but in the socially inclined baboons maternal care can be less strong. A chimp, or a baboon infant in the situation of the other would be lost.

That there can be great variety within one order or even within one family of animals is also noted; hence the danger of generalizing within even one family. It may be that the capacity to adjust by replacing one method by another is greatest in the higher vertebrates and is put to its maximum use in man.

It should be noted that fathering in the animal kingdom is an entity as well defined as mothering − if the term 'instinct' is employed it would apply as much to fathering as to mothering.

The lessons for man are obvious − parenting is more important than parents. To have loving care for the young is the essential thing. Man has devised a very effective way of bringing up children − in a group of people, the family. In most circumstances it works very well and among its advantages are its flexibility. The concept of the family now calls for attention.

FAMILIES NURTURE CHILDREN

Man employs the family as the caring unit for his children. Or does he? Are children not cared for by mother? To demonstrate that this latter view is fallacious is the point of this section. Even the obvious will have to be shown to be true by statistics − or the obvious will not be accepted.

Families make more families. The child is the representative from the family of the present to the family of the future. He is an integral part of the first family and carries his personal ingredients with him into the future one. Moreover, this child is nurtured in his impressionable and formative years by the whole family.

Western culture has tended to overlook the fact that the child is brought up in a group situation, the family, and has given undue emphasis to one element in the group, maternal care. It is an unusual situation for an infant or child to relate to his mother alone, even in the first few days of life. In the nuclear family, the child relates to father, mother and siblings; but nuclear families are infrequently as small as this, and in addition often have within them grandparents, parental siblings, friends, servants and the child's peers. The contribution of each member of a group to the infant is variable; mother may be paramount in giving care; less often father may have the major role − or a grandparent, a relative, or a sibling. The care given by any family member, including mother, may be constructive or destructive, depending on their personal qualities and the meaning of the child to them. To be part of a group gives the child protection; what one member of the group lacks in his care may be supplied by another; for Homo sapiens, nature did not 'put all its eggs in one basket'.

To prove the obvious, that children are brought up by the whole family, we must refer to two studies.

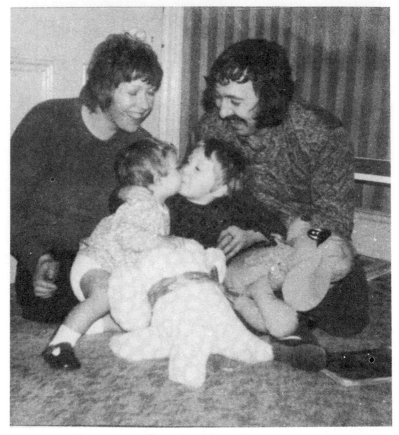

Figure 5 – A happy family

Study one – the Ipswich thousand family survey

This study has yet to be published in its entirety but a brief account has been given by this author in *Principles of Family Psychiatry,* to be published shortly. A briefer account is given here. The object of the study was to see who related to children from birth up to the age of ten. The crucial findings for our purposes are found in Table 1.

By studying a random sample of 100 children in each year of age up to ten years, making a total of about 1,000 children, for the ten-year age spread, it was possible by time sampling and the use of a computer to establish the percentage of relating time between the child and all other possible humans during a 24-hour period. Relating is defined as the position of one person with respect to another and offering the possibility of communication. The 1,000 families are a random sample selected from birth records. The findings for each year for the first ten years are to be found in Table 1. It should be noted that 'relating time' is greater than 'actual time'. as of course relating can go on with a number of people at the same time.

TABLE 1
Pattern of Relating over 24 Hours
(Given in Percentages
By Age of Child)

Age, years	Mother	Father	Siblings	Adult Relatives	Others	Acquaintances	Peers out of School	Peers and Teachers	Alone	Asleep
1	25.84	12.10	12.81	6.79	0.71	2.58	1.53	0.06	0.47	37.09 *
2	26.72	12.05	16.26	6.19	0.02	4.10	2.54	0.04	0.39	31.67
3	25.99	12.97	20.03	6.29	0.20	2.91	2.23	0.08	0.40	28.90
4	25.16	13.62	21.27	4.54	0.46	3.61	2.63	0.74	0.39	27.57
5	26.85	12.25	19.97	5.02	0.44	4.15	1.92	0.56	0.66	28.17
6	21.38	12.57	19.32	3.82	0.21	3.06	2.81	7.84	0.55	28.44
7	22.50	12.85	17.94	4.45	0.01	3.22	2.35	7.29	0.66	28.72
8	20.38	13.64	19.27	3.18	0.18	3.42	2.68	8.39	0.47	28.39
9	19.04	13.02	18.87	2.98	0.09	3.69	2.65	10.81	0.72	28.13
10	19.89	11.88	19.58	4.60	0.00	4.12	3.78	7.92	0.84	27.39
Average	23.45	12.71	18.62	4.79	0.24	3.49	2.51	4.27	0.55	29.37

The first and clearest conclusion that can be drawn from the table (Table 1) is that the child during these impressionable first ten years relates to a number of people — mother, father, siblings, relatives in the home, others in the home, acquaintances outside the home, peers outside the home, and others at school. It is equally clear that this fact of the child's relating to a number of people is also relevant in the first five years and even in the first year.

Most of the time is spent in the home, for the whole 10 years 89.27 per cent of the time (including sleeping time). In the first year this amounts to 95.34 per cent of the 24 hours. It can be seen that the mother, father and siblings are the main relaters in the home, while adult relatives are a significant influence also. On calculation of the averages the mother was found to be the longest relater accounting for 23.45 per cent of the relating time, the siblings came next with 18.62 per cent of the time and father next with 12.71 per cent of relating time. In view of the prominence given to the mother–child relationship it is very important to note that this is considerably less in duration than that of the rest of the family, 23.45 per cent compared

TABLE 2
Pattern of Relating According to Time of Day
(in Percentages)

Time	Mother	Father	Siblings	Adult Relatives	Others	Acquaintances	Peers out of School	Peers and Teachers	Alone	Asleep
Morning	28.78	14.72	23.47	2.40	0.19	0.69	0.81	1.81	1.33	25.81
Day	31.76	15.16	25.02	7.42	0.35	6.10	4.29	8.18	0.09	1.63
Evening	19.23	16.05	16.15	4.06	0.19	1.96	1.47	0.01	1.62	39.26
Night	1.16	0.61	0.07	0.04	0.00	0.01	0.00	0.00	0.06	98.05
Average	23.45	12.71	18.62	4.79	0.24	3.49	2.51	4.27	0.55	29.37

with 36.36 per cent. The mother is the longest single relater, but the rest of the family collectively have a far longer relating time. In the first year the same appertains, 25.84 per cent, as against 32.41 per cent. The proportion of mother relating to all relating (in and out of home) is 23.45:46.63, i.e. 1:2.

The fact that father spent less time with his children is due not so much to his lack of interest, as to lack of opportunity, as a result of being the main breadwinner in the community under study; this is supported by the fact that in the evening his time approximates to that of mother: 16.05 per cent (Table 2) as against 19.23 per cent, i.e. 83 per cent of mother's time. This increases on Saturday (Table 3) and on Sunday amounts to 80 per cent of the time spent by mother. Father's time spent with his children was similar in all income groups with a slight increase in the higher income group and a small drop in the lower group.

TABLE 3
Pattern of Relating According to Day of the Week
(Given in Percentages)

Day of Week	Mother	Father	Siblings	Adult Relatives	Others	Acquaintances	Peers out of School	Peers and Teachers	Alone	Asleep
Monday	24.33	11.36	18.12	4.37	0.15	3.43	2.54	5.37	0.65	29.68
Tuesday	23.20	5.26	17.21	4.20	0.76	3.14	2.35	7.46	0.57	31.84
Wednesday	22.56	9.49	18.24	4.73	0.45	3.67	2.60	7.02	0.44	30.81
Thursday	23.34	11.05	17.11	5.76	0.00	4.07	2.79	5.12	0.47	30.29
Friday	23.98	10.60	17.61	4.34	0.14	3.54	2.16	5.93	0.49	31.20
Saturday	23.36	16.78	21.36	4.37	0.02	3.81	3.22	0.02	0.49	26.56
Sunday	23.38	18.71	20.09	5.63	0.18	2.86	1.95	0.26	0.73	26.22
Average	23.45	12.71	18.62	4.79	0.24	3.49	2.51	4.27	0.55	29.37

An important finding that emerges from Table 1 is that father's relating time with his children is not significantly less in the first two years. Contemporary psychoanalytical theory maintains that father is not a significant factor in the first two years and that when contact occurs, he takes on a 'mothering role'. The facts suggest that the father's influence is direct, as strong as in any other group and consists of himself in a fathering role rather than any qualities borrowed from his wife.

An interesting finding was the amount of time spent relating to siblings. For the first ten years this amounted to 18.62 per cent (Table 1) of the day and was not much less than the time spent with the mother. The significance of the influence of child upon child has been grossly underestimated in the literature in contemporary child care.

That mother, siblings and father should account for the majority of the relating time emphasizes the importance of the nuclear family in child care, especially as it is by far the commonest type of family.

It could be argued, that, while it appears that father, brothers and sisters together relate to the child for a longer period than the mother alone, the concentration of care given by the mother is greater. Another study looks into this question.

Study two — concentration of care

Relating offers the possibility of interaction with another person, but does not of itself tell us how much use is made of the time for interaction. It could be argued that some members of the family circle were more active in making use of communication and therefore they would be of greater significance in having an effect upon another family member. It was possible to study this feature of relating in an allied investigation which will now be reported.

By great good fortune an American study is available which made a very exacting investigation of 24 hours in the life of a boy aged seven years. So detailed are the data that it is possible to make an accurate measurement of the amount of relating time spent with each possible object, furthermore, to make an estimation of the amount of communication between the boy and the same object. By comparing the second chart with the first it was possible to ascertain the use made of relating time for communication and thus estimate the concentration of interaction given by the relating persons.

This study, *One Boy's Day* by Barker and Wright*, is astonishing in its detail, reporting for one day the minute-by-minute life of a boy aged 7 in an American town. The authors of the book offer no analysis or interpretation of their observations; they merely report the facts. However, so detailed is the study, that it has been possible for us to determine from the facts reported (1) the number of minutes of physical contact between the child and those around him, and (2) the active use the child made of this physical contact with others around him as a means of communication.

One waking day, consisting of 813 minutes, was chosen for observation in the life of this child in a small American Mid-West town. It was a weekday, Tuesday, in 1949, during the time of the year when the child was attending school. The period of waking time was 7.0 a.m. to 8.33

*Barker, R. G. and Wright, H. F. (1966). *One Boy's Day, a specimen record of behaviour.* New York; Harper and Row p.m., i.e. 813 minutes. Eight observers were chosen, seven of them well known to the boy. They each had an observational period of approximately 30 minutes and each recorded every fact and impression in a minute-by-minute diary. Everything the boy did and spoke was dictated into a tape recorder by the observer on the task. In addition the boy's body movements were recorded, and attempts were made to interpret his thoughts. The tape was then played back to another person who queried any unclear passages, until a final clear script was achieved. This was transcribed in the form of a minute-by-minute observation throughout the day. The transcription, without interpretation, was first published as a book, in 1951.

After a careful analysis of *One Boy's Day* it was possible for us to list all the people and animals, within and without the boy's home, who had physical proximity with him on the day of the study. Having listed the living objects to whom he related, it was possible to extract from the data the exact amount spent by each object in proximity to the boy, the observers being excluded. The total relating time was then calculated and a Chart of Relating was produced.

Further careful study of the data on the criteria below produced a Chart of Communication, i.e., the minutes of physical relating which the boy used for communication with each object were calculated.

Furthermore, by comparing the two charts it was possible to calculate the percentage of relating time used for communication with each object, i.e., the use made of the relationship.

Relating and communicating are different entities. Relating offers the possibility of communication, but the individual may or may not make use of his opportunity. At this point it may be useful to discuss how relating and communication are defined. It should be noted that the same definitions are accepted for each person; if these definitions are limited for one person, they are also limited for another and thus comparison between persons are valid within the criteria employed.

The term *relationship* denotes the passive standing of one person to another. A chart of relating shows to whom the subject relates and for how long. Two persons can turn this situation of relating into a *communication;* this describes the active process of associating between people. A chart of communication records with whom the subject communicates and for how long.

The intensity of communicating must also be taken into account. Many meanings can be conveyed during communication; some subtle and almost indiscernible, some discernible with ease, and some blatantly obvious. In the first category might come a father who sits with his family at a meal without exchanging a word with them; yet his presence influences the family. Into the second category might come an

ordinary conversation around the meal table. In the third would come a
heated argument between members of a family. The analysis of the data
in *One Boy's Day* could embrace safely only the second and third
categories. As the first category was excluded, it is likely that more
communication took place than is recorded. However, comparisons of
communication between different persons can safely be made within
these criteria as the same criteria for communication was adopted for
all interactions.

It can be seen from Table 4 that the greatest use of relating time for
communication was made in the case of his friends outside school (78.9
per cent), with animals (69.7 per cent), with neighbours (64.4 per
cent), with mother (53.6 per cent) and father (50 per cent). It is of

TABLE 4

Percentage use made of Relating Time for Communicating

Object	Time in minutes	Percentage of relating time
Father	56/112	50
Mother	82/153	53.6
Neighbours	9/14	64.4
Friends outside school	71/90	78.9
Friends in school	90/299	30.1
School teachers	44/229	19.2
Courthouse staff and other adults	15/37	40.5
Animals	30/43	69.7
Alone	108/108	100
Total use of 'relating time'	505/1085	46.5 (including self communication)
Use of relating time for communicating	397/1085	36.6 (communication to others only)
Total use of 'Waking time'	397/813	48.8 (communication to others only)

some importance to note that, on the basis of the criteria employed, to
the fine communication, the use made of communication during the
relating time was almost identical for mother and father.

It could be reasonably argued that, although longer communication
takes place for instance with his peers (19.8 per cent of his waking

day), the communications with his parents (17 per cent of his waking day) may be more significant for his personality development, in that they reinforce impressions that have existed between his parents and himself for seven years. This would be as true for his father as for his mother and for siblings, had he had any. If the same proportions of relating and communicating had existed throughout his seven years as did on this typical day, it would seem that father's influence was hardly less than that of the mother. The concentration of influence from siblings could not be measured in this study as he was the sole child in the family.

Implications of studies

The implications of the above works, the *Ipswich Thousand Family Survey* and the analysis of *One Boy's Day,* are far reaching.

In the *Ipswich Thousand Family Survey,* the obvious is statistically confirmed — children are nurtured by families. The child relates to a number of people. From conception onward the child is part of a group of people of much significance to one another. As an active participator in a polydynamic open system, he gains and loses from the continual transaction, depending on the quality of that transaction. He cannot be understood apart from the group and the transaction, and he is destined to carry their influence on into the future.

The analysis of *One Boy's Day* shows that the use of relating time for communication within the family is virtually the same for father and mother.

The biological advantage to the individual is obvious. If he were to be condemned to a need and an ability to relate to one person alone, then, having lost that person, his life would be over. Furthermore, what he may lose in one relationship he may gain in another; the defects of one parent are compensated by the other, or by a relative, a sibling, or a nanny.

The theory of the necessity of one unique object relationship, and that being with his mother, is no longer tenable. A child needs his family, including his mother. In our society, due to the economic situation, mother may give more care than any other family member, but it would be a shallow experience, lacking richness, to be tied to her alone. Mothers vary in this capacity to relate to others, including children. So do other family members. But to centre child care on the whole family allows one family member to compensate for any deficiencies another may have in relating to children. A number of good relationships are better than one. A number of nice mothers is even better than one nice mother.

The founders of future families, it seems, spend the major part of their time in the family. It is strikingly apparent that the home is the predominent milieu of a child. In the first five years it amounts to 93.56 per cent of relating time including sleep; it is less in children over five (84.60 per cent) and for the whole ten years amount to 89.18 per cent of relating time. Thus we have to look for the causes of good emotional health or psychonosis (neurosis) in the heart of the family.

The above studies underline also the importance of siblings. They contribute a large amount of relating time, almost as great as the mother. The child in *One Boy's Day* had no siblings but if children in the home use relating to the same degree as peers outside (the highest concentration of care in the above investigation), then their impact on one another must be a major factor in family life. Parents claim recognition of their contribution to children; siblings are less able to ask for theirs. We cannot omit the same careful evaluation of their contribution to family life. At a new birth in the family the feelings of any existing children are immediately engaged.

Psychoanalysts have gone on record to maintain that the first two years of a child's life is not a period that calls for participation by fathers. The facts published here disprove this contention. Fathers are involved in conception, a positive and essential contribution. They share the anticipation or strain of pregnancy; increasingly they wish to share the joy of the moment of birth. They are full participants from the moment of birth and communicate as freely as mother.

Fathers deserve more consideration. For a long time mother has been given her proper place as an important influence in the care of children. Unjustly, father's place has been played down — especially by the experts, strangely enough. A special section here will be devoted to the contribution the father makes in the care of children; it will restore the balance and show him as an equal partner alongside the mother. Both parents, and others, are carers of children and all of them, if they can love, can contribute to their successful upbringing.

FATHERING

Introduction

Fathering is an element in family life as distinct as mothering. Yet legal enactions, social policy and art forms in Western culture, although not in all cultures, neglect fathering in comparison to mothering. The neglect of fathering is at its greatest in contemporary child psychiatry and psychology. In fact the father can be a major influence in health or pathology. Maria, after all, lived with her stepfather as well as with her mother. It would appear that he was the main disturbing element in her life. It was he who killed her.

Our earlier excursion into animal behaviour showed that if there is such a thing as a mothering instinct, then there is also a fathering

Figure 6 — A happy scene with a child and her father

instinct. A truer statement would be to say that many people have a potential capacity to care for the young. The capacity to care for the human infant is possessed by many people and the most significant roles have been given, although not exclusively, to his family members. A father's feelings are real, deep, tender, warm and concerned — just as are those of the mother. Let Shakespeare remind us of the strong feelings of fathers. These sad and poignant lines were written shortly after the death of his son Hamnet.

> Grief fills the room up of my absent child,
> Lies in his bed, walks up and down with me,
> Puts on his pretty looks, repeats his words,
> Remembers me of all his gracious parts,
> Stuffs out his vacant garments with his form:
>
> . . . .
>
> O Lord! my boy, my Arthur, my fair son!
> My life, my joy, my food, my all the world!
>
> (*King John,* III, iv, 93–97 and 103–104)

Some psychoanalytical writers do not regard fathering as an element in family life as distinct as mothering. In this connection, Ackerman stated: 'I am inclined to believe that there is no separate fathering instinct.' Proponents of this point of view regard any tender, kind, solicitous care of the infant by father as 'mothering'. This carries the implication that such behaviour by men is not masculine – yet it is regarded as a virtue in the marriage relationship. The same view regards these qualities as borrowed from, or an imitation of, the mother and not intrinsic to the father.

Again this viewpoint tends to emphasize the biological function of the mother in child care – that she alone bears and breast feeds the child. Furthermore, it is assumed that father is a latecomer to the child's life, arriving on the scene only when the child begins to talk and be independent. All these views can be challenged.

The author asserts that fathering is an element in family life as significant as mothering. Fathering and mothering may have many components; most are probably in common, a few may be dissimilar. There are more likenesses in mothering and fathering than there are differences. Both are the product of an intimate emotional experience with their own parents of both sexes; they must absorb components from both. Both also have much in common with relatedness elsewhere – foster parenting, adoptive parenting, marital relatedness, grand-parenting, etc. A child in his tender years requires this protective relatedness from any source; normally, it is given equally by father and mother, sometimes better by father or mother, and sometimes better by others.

Again, to emphasize mother's biological role in bearing the infant is to overlook the psychological climate of conception and pregnancy. The acceptance of father by mother may be the predominant factor in leading to the acceptance of a child from him, and uniquely from him. Thereafter the parents become a pair linked in a common endeavour, in which, however, only one of them can physically bear the yet unborn child. The father's thoughts, feelings and actions influence the mother's regard to her child and thus indirectly the child. Striking evidence of the father's involvement is seen in the couvade syndrome.

The first child emerges into an already formed psychological group situation of father, mother and child. The group of a second child is a larger one, consisting of four people. The child may be introduced to the group in any order — often he meets father first, if the mother is incapacitated. Thereafter, what he receives from each member of the group is dependent on their feelings for him, their capacity for relating, and the roles given them. This is infinitely variable and unique for each family. The one thing that a father cannot do for his child is to breast feed him (although there are isolated instances of the child being soothed at his father's nipples). In the contemporary bottle-feeding society, this is not the handicap that it might appear. All else a father can do directly for his child. When not directly participating in his care, the father still influences his child through his intimate relationship with the mother; after all, a father normally regards a child as a tangible evidence of his own union with the mother. The child is fortunate in the insurance of two parents, whereby one can compensate for the other. Father supports mother and child; equally, mother supports father and child. The part played by a particular father, or a particular mother, is dependent on their own previous family, clan and social experiences.

Already we have seen from our consideration of animal behaviour how fathering can be the predominent type of caring employed in nature in some circumstances. Anthropology also demonstrates how fathering in some societies is given more prominence than in our own.

Anthropology

Each culture imagines its way of child rearing and family life to be the best. An appraisal of history and of many cultures today shows how varied are family patterns and child care practices. As in the animal kingdom, nature is more concerned that the human child should have the required care than she is about the way in which the care is given; over the latter, she displays variety and flexibility. Her main instrument for child nurture is a group, the family. Fathering, within the group, is not neglected, as will now be demonstrated.

Amongst the Arapesh, for instance, Mead states that the father plays an equal part with the mother during pregnancy. The child is thought of as the product of father's semen and mother's blood. The child's conception is a joint endeavour, and during the early weeks of pregnancy, following the cessation of menstruation, the father 'works' to produce his child by strenuous sexual activity with his wife. His involvement with mother and infant after the child's birth is so close as to earn the phrase that he is 'in bed having a baby'. The child's strength is also thought to be dependent on the father, who is forbidden sexual intercourse until the child can walk and is then believed strong enough to withstand the parents' sexuality again. The care of children is regarded as the task of both men and women.

Again, on the island of Manua, in the Admiralty Islands, Mead reports that the father is the dominant and the tender, loving parent. After the birth of her first child, the mother lives with her family. Then she returns to her husband's house and from the first he takes a fiercely possessive interest in the child, male or female. As soon as the child can stand, the father takes the child from the mother. She is set to work, while he spends all the time left free from his fishing with the child. The child is his constant companion and at night sleeps with him (the female child until she is seven or eight years old). The second-born gives mother a child for a few months, but, at this time, the first-born moves even closer to his father. The life of all the children is around the father, whether he be their natural or adoptive father. There is a strong personality resemblance between the adopted children and their adoptive father.

As often appertains in primitive societies, should the social economy require father and sons to work together, then father may exert a great influence on the upbringing of sons, and mothers, conversely, on the upbringing of their daughters.

Not only do anthropological studies demonstrate instances of exclusive paternal care, but they challenge, too, an over-rigid definition of the qualities required in 'masculinity' and 'femininity'. Mead quotes her experiences in New Guinea. The Arapesh ideal of a man is that he should be mild and responsive; the Arapesh ideal woman should be the same. The Mundugumer ideal is that of a violent aggressive male and female. The Tchambuli reverse what we commonly regard as masculine and feminine attitudes – their ideal woman is dominant, impersonal and managing, while the man is dependent, art loving and unmanaging.

Social anthropology reveals the same variability and flexibility in the care of the young as in the animal kingdom. What is appropriate in a given situation is the means employed. The family group is paramount, and within it fathering has an important place; in a particular milieu there may even be exclusive care by the father.

Fathering in contemporary society

Father is largely neglected in contemporary social literature on the family in most countries, and the available literature concentrates on a few aspects of fathering only. There is support for the idea that the absence of father may have an adverse effect on the family. This carries the implication that he means something when present. The literature suggests that he plays a part in child development, but authorities disagree about its nature. Some see father as secondary in the contemporary family, while others give him a more powerful role. Some direct studies suggest that his participation is greater than expected.

The Newsons, for instance, found a high degree of participation by fathers in the lives of the children they observed. They found that 57 per cent of Social Class I and II (upper professional) fathers were highly participant, 61 per cent of Social Class III (white collar), 51 per cent of Social Class III (skilled manual), 55 per cent of Social Class IV and 36 per cent of Social Class V (unskilled).

Again, Gavron, in a sample of middle class parents, found 44 per cent of the fathers would do and, in fact, did everything required for their children from playing with them to soothing them when they cried at night, from feeding them to changing their nappies. A further 21 per cent were rated very helpful by their wives, which meant they would do most things as a matter of course, but drew the line at one or two things, usually changing nappies. Of the wives, 31 per cent rated their husbands as interested but not helpful. Only 4 per cent of the wives in the entire sample rated their husbands as non-participant.

In working-class families, Gavron found, as with the middle-class families, that the degree to which the father participated in the lives of his children was quite striking, and the degree of participation was even greater than among the middle-class families. Of fathers, 52 per cent were rated by their wives as doing anything and everything for their children as a matter of course. A further 27 per cent were prepared to do most things, drawing the line as did some middle-class fathers over changing nappies, and getting up at night. Of the remainder (21 per cent) 12 per cent were considered 'interested but not helpful' and just over half to be uninvolved in their children's lives.

Precise figures are available on the extent of fathering from the previously mentioned *Ipswich One Thousand Family Survey*. Table 1 shows the pattern of relating by mother and father in each year of the child's life up to the age of ten years. Some obvious conclusions emerge.

(1) Father's relating amounts to an average of 12.71 per cent of the child's relating time during 24 hours during the whole 10 years; mother's period of relating is twice father's relating time.

(2) Father's relating time amounts to approximately the same per

cent for every year including the first year of the child's first ten years. Mother's contribution tends to decline with the years. This does not support the common contention that father is less interested in his children in the first two years.

A question that could be asked is whether the father is less interested in his children than the mother or whether he has less opportunity by the nature of our economic system which dictates that fathers are more often at work than mothers. The latter contention is supported by the figures relating to the time of day: in the evening mother's percentage of relating time fell from 23.45 per cent for the whole day to 19.23 per cent while father's contribution rose from his average for the day of 12.71 per cent to 16.05 per cent. Again, when the figures for the day of the week are considered it is seen that father's percentage of the child's relating time increases from the average of 12.71 per cent for the whole week to 18.71 per cent on Sundays. Indeed, on Sundays it is only just short of mother's percentage of relating time (23.38 per cent). We can conclude that, given the opportunity, father appears almost as interested as mother and shows no less interest in the first few years.

It is questionable whether fathering is a recent phenomenon. However, some writers have assumed a recent increase in fathering, and give a number of reasons for the change. It is argued that the small modern home brings the child closer to father; but the poorer classes have always lived in small houses. The absence of servants, they argue, forces the father to help mother with the children; but most families have never had servants. That mother now tends to work, they contend, forces father to help; but in many societies women have always worked. It is thought that equality of the sexes may make the modern woman independent of her husband, and thus able to demand help from him. Furthermore, she sees her role in terms not too different from his; thus sharing of roles is more possible. Affluence in society calls for less hours of work, and father can participate more readily in family life. It should be noted that, in varying degrees at different times, these reasons have always applied in some societies.

As we have seen, the neglect of father in the literature on contemporary society is striking; the most common assumption is that child care is matricentric. The above direct studies and the *Ipswich Thousand Family Survey* suggest that father participation is much greater than expected.

Neglect of father's contribution

Reasons for this neglect in the Western world may be several. In the Christian religion a far more prominent place is given to Christ's mother, Mary, in His upbringing than is accorded to His father, Joseph. The Madonna and Child have been a frequent subject for the artist in the last 1,900 years; Joseph and Child are rarely depicted.

Again, by tradition in the Western world, the man assumes the main role of breadwinner, while the woman has charge of home and children. This may help to explain how, where women traditionally work, e.g. in Russia, parenting is more likely to be a shared responsibility.

The tendency for mothers to accompany children to child welfare clinics may lead to neglect of fathers and the assumption that the mother alone is involved in the child's problem.

The fact that professional workers in the children's field are frequently women may introduce a bias by their empathy with the female parent.

More subtle childhood influences on these professional workers in the Western world may set up a preoccupation with the mother – especially the idealization of the mother. Again, selection factors may be operating to bring into the field of child care less well-adjusted individuals who would assume that their anomalous backgrounds are characteristic of family life generally. There may also be selection in terms of social class; child care workers may come from backgrounds where servants, and thus less participation by fathers, were common.

Earlier mention has been made of the consequences of ignoring the father in estimating the pathology of the family. He is often the last to be approached if a child is emotionally or physically ill. As father is less available, it is assumed that he is less interested and arrangements, such as appointment times, are made which make it difficult for him to be seen.

Legal provisions have yet to give father a just place when guardianship of children is considered at divorce; the needs and rights of the unmarried father have been given even less consideration.

Conclusion

It is maintained here, supported by evidence, that fathering and mothering are equally important and complementary in the caring of children. Loving care may be a quality in both parents; happily, this is often so. Loving care may be found in a greater degree in one of the parents rather than in the other. When this happens, there is much to be said for that parent to taken on the main direct parenting role, supported by the other parent. Flexibility of role often happens and is to be encouraged. Tender loving care is as much an attribute of men as it is of women. In both it is dependent on experiences in their own childhood, rather than upon genetic endowment. Both mothering and fathering are only a part, though an important one, of total care by a group, the family.

In normal circumstances, care in the natural family is the best way of guaranteeing that the child's essential requirement, loving care, is satisfied. Should the family fail, for a number of reasons, to supply this care, it has to be obtained elsewhere. Caring is more important than the method employed. Thus we now turn to consider forms of substitute care.

SUBSTITUTE CARE

Children cannot choose to which set of people they are born. But people do wish to produce their own children wherever possible. This last fact makes it right to leave children in the care of their parents unless the rights of the child are prejudiced. This interest of parents in their own children is an asset and an asset well worth using. The parents' interest in their own children usually turns around their feelings about their spouse – nurturing an epitome of the other, a common endeavour in something conceived together, and a continuing common interest. There are other reasons that weight heavily with some parents: supposed genetic advantages, the carrying on of family traits, the perpetuation of themselves through children, etc.

It is worth reflecting that research into adoption shows that those parents who love their children most are also those most successful with adopted children. As we have said above, loving care in many people extends far beyond their own children and in some instances can embrace almost any child.

I recall a man who came to see me with his wife who was seeking help with her fourth confinement. Only the first child was his own. The other three children were by other men. He had changed his employment so that he could stay at home during the day to look after the children while his wife went to work. She came home in the evening to baby-sit while he went to work. When asked how and why he could care for these children, he said, 'Well, you see, someone has to bring them up and I like children. My wife doesn't love me, I know, but I love her.' Such capacity is not unusual or strange. People adjust to situations and then they do not need professional help. When they fail to adjust, they come for help. Thus it is easily possible for helpers to fail to see the extraordinary adjustments, flexible arrangements, changes of role and compromises going on around them. People study riots, sickness, and disasters. They do not study tranquility, health and adjustment.

The human heart is big and at times astonishingly all-embracing. An

Figure 7 – A foster child is reunited with his foster mother

active young and successful business executive had just married and in no time his wife was pregnant. He was delighted. She was depressed. When her depression became serious, she was sent to me. After obtaining her confidence (and those who doubt the need for confidentiality should reflect on this case history), she was able to disclose the reason for her depression. There are always reasons for depression, but some intimate, shattering, and embarrassing events are not easy to talk about. She said, 'You see, the child is not my husband's'. It seems that senior to her husband in the firm was a coloured man against whom she had no prejudice, but against whom her husband, due to his background, had violent hatred because of his race. The two men also clashed as personalities. The man's very name aroused wrath in her husband. And now she carried this coloured man's child. It all happened so casually. She was not yet committed to her husband and slept with the other man. The experience confirmed that her husband was the man for her. But in a short while she found herself pregnant – and after her husband had proposed to her. In a panic she clung to him and consented to his eagerness for an early marriage. It was clear that her husband must be told the truth. But she could not tell him nor permit anyone else to do so. Week by week time went by. She hoped for some miracle. It never came, but the child did – and she found that he was the same colour as his father. She still could not bring herself to tell her husband. Minute by minute he was kept at bay despite his eagerness to see his child. At last she knew that the truth had to be told. And all her husband said was, 'Well he is your child, isn't he? So he is mine too. Aren't we lucky to have a child so soon'. This was an exceptional case, but often exceptions are not so rare as we assume.

People, then, have a capacity to love children – their own and other people's children. They just love children. This capacity is present in all – fortunate parents and others. The others are no different from parents. Indeed, they often become parents. The capacity to love children is not something that arrives together with the birth of the child. It is there before – in most of us, parents or not. Indeed it is this capacity that encourages us to conceive children. Some people, however, have the capacity to love, but, for many reasons, cannot conceive. The reasons that prevent conception – being unmarried, infertility, physical conditions etc. – are separate from the capacity to love. If the capacity to love children is there, but cannot find expression in maternity or paternity, it remains available for the children of others. Substitute parenting is not essentially different from parenting. Indeed parenting and substitute parenting are often undertaken by the same person, a school teacher who is a father or a mother, the staff of a children's home who are parents, or foster parents or adoptive parents who have children of their own.

Substitute parents are no better nor worse than natural parents. They are just people, of whom most have much capacity for caring, some are indifferent carers, and some care not at all. However, in practice, there is one important difference between natural and substitute parents. A child cannot choose his own parents, but his substitute parents can be chosen for him. Thus, given wise choosing, a child should have an advantage in always having caring parents. Regrettably, the procedures we have in this field as yet lack precision.

That others can love children is of immense help to our children. So wonderful to have so many nice daddys — uncle, older brother Bill, grandpa, teacher, my pal's father. So wonderful to have so many nice mummys — auntie, older sister Kay, grandma, teacher, my pal's mother. And substitute parents can be such a protection to our children in adversity if we make good use of them. The child needs loving care. Denied it in his own home (and never can a home be truly blamed) he can have it elsewhere, if we allow him to.

The range of possible substitute parents is wide. Complete care can be given by adoptive parents, foster parents, relatives, a nanny in the higher income groups, and the staff of cottage homes. For shorter periods care can be given by the staff of hostels, of boarding schools and of hospital units. Naturally, the more intense and intimate the care, the better it is. A good adoption is to be preferred to a hostel. But a good hostel is preferable to a poor adoption. The quality of the loving care that can be given is the essential matter. Partial substitute care can be offered by baby-minders, day nurseries, play groups, nursery schools, day schools, etc. Many of these we shall consider later in this book.

When parents fail, children must turn to others, and sometimes they are fortunate. Winston Churchill acknowledged his indebtedness to his nanny, Mrs. Everest. Winston became her charge soon after his birth and was virtually never separated from her for eight years, even to the extent of sharing her room. Winston was to say of her in his *My Early Life* 'My nurse was my confidante. Mrs. Everest it was who looked after me and tended all my wants. It was to her I poured out my many troubles.' It is said that during a walk at Chartwell he turned to his son Randolph saying, 'Do you realize that you have just spent more time with me than I spent with my father in my lifetime?' His parents were remote; Mrs. Everest everpresent. Of his mother he said, 'I loved her dearly — but at a distance.' In his novel *Savrola* the two women reappear, the distant unobtainable young beauty and the faithful loving old woman. His comments on the latter are revealing.

She waited on him, plying him the while with questions and watching his appetite with anxious pleasure. She had nursed him from his birth up with a devotion and care which knew no break. It is a strange thing, the love of these women. Perhaps it is the only disinterested affection in the world. The mother loves her child; that is maternal nature. The youth loves his sweetheart; that too may be explained. The dog loves his master; he feeds him; a man loves his friend; he has stood by him perhaps at doubtful moments. In all there are reasons; but the love of a foster-mother for her charge appears absolutely irrational. It is one of the few proofs, not to be explained even by the association of ideas, that the nature of mankind is superior to mere utilitarianism, and that his destinies are high.

Her perfect trust in her idol had banished all fears on her own account, but she had 'fidgeted terribly' about him. He was all she had in the world; others dissipate their affections on a husband, children, brothers, and sisters; all the love of her kind old heart was centred in the man she had fostered since he was a helpless baby. And he did not forget.

His love of Kent and his subsequent settlement there must have been due to Mrs. Everest. 'I was also taught to be fond of Kent. It was, Mrs. Everest said, "the garden of England". I always wanted to live in Kent.'

When Mrs. Everest's services were to be dispensed with, what Winston called 'to be cut adrift', he had this to say, 'I should be very sorry not to have her at Grosvenor Square — because she is in my mind associated — more than anything else — with *home*'. She was not well treated by the family, but he made her an allowance. In Parliament he supported old age pensions and said, 'When I think of the fate of poor old women, so many of whom have no-one to look after them and nothing to live on at the end of their lives, I am gland to have had a hand in all that structure of pensions and insurance.'

When Mrs. Everest was on her deathbed he did all that a son could do and commented 'She had been my dearest and most intimate friend during the whole of the twenty years I had lived. I shall never known such a friend again.' He and his brother erected a memorial to her and paid an annual sum to the local florist for the upkeep of the grave.

Edith Sitwell too needed substitute care and got love from a governess and from a peacock, as she recalls in *Taken Care Of.* Her life started in turmoil.

My grandmother stormed, bringing about my early arrival into the world by this singularly appalling row.

'I have wondered sometimes', my mother said, recalling this occasion, 'whether this violence was because you were trying to be born, or whether you were wanting to get at your grandmother.'

My mother ran away a few days after the marriage, and returned to her parents. But my grandmother sent her back. Changeling that I am, I was born nine months after that slavery began. No wonder that my mother hated me throughout my childhood and youth.

Marital bliss was far away and her mother wished to be free; she would say, 'Of course, what I would really like, would be to get your father put in a lunatic asylum.'

The child was not acceptable.

I was unpopular with my parents from the moment of my birth, and throughout my childhood and youth, I was in disgrace for being a female.

My parents were strangers to me from the moment of my birth. I do not forget that I must have been a most exasperating child, living with violence each moment of my day.

Love came from elsewhere – her governess; 'My friends were my dear old nurse Davis. (When I think of her now, I see her like a phrase in my friend Gertrude Stein's *Geography and Plays*, "a shadow, a white shadow, is a mountain". She was at once a white shadow and a mountain. And her real name was comfort.)' and a valet; 'And my other friend – my father's valet Henry Moat – whose friendship with my brothers and me lasted until his death', and a peacock; 'On our return to Renishaw, I concentrated my love on the Renishaw peacock. This love was, at the time, returned. He would wait for me until I left my mother's room, then, with another harsh shriek, would fly down into the large gardens. We walked round these, with my arm round his lovely nook, that shone like tears in the dark forest.'

Of her father she had this to say: 'He rarely spoke to the members of his family, or to visitors, seeming, indeed, to be separated from them by an endless plain – a stretch of centuries, perhaps, a continent with all its differences of climate, or the enormous space that divides these.'

About her feelings for her mother, she made perhaps the most bitter comment in all literature:

The Hume children were of about the same age as myself, four or five.

One afternoon, after I had not seen them for some time, Davis and I went to tea with them. They seemed shadowed beings, dressed in black.

Their mother was generally present at nursery tea, but on this occasion, she was not there, and I asked where she was. They cried bitterly. 'She is dead' they said. Soon afterwards, we left, not staying for the usual after-tea-time games. I asked Davis why they had cried.

'Because their mother is dead.'

'Yes, I know. But why did they cry?'

SUMMARY AND CONCLUSION

Loving care is more important than the means by which it is supplied. Parenting is more important than parents. But parents have the first right to parent a child if they can give loving care, as most of them can. Natural mothering is precious. So is fathering. So also is an upbringing in a warm happy family. The family rears children. The family provides the loving care. The family has advantages over any one individual parent.

The child strives to survive, but cannot be sure of it. Thus nature has supplied him with the security and help of a group, a family group, a security enhanced by its not being dependent on one person alone. His personality is flavoured and moulded by a number of interdependent individuals who form part of a complex whole, a polydynamic system, the family group, the situation. From his family the child learns the essential lesson of marriage, parenting and family life. His success will be his family's success, his failure theirs. Harmonious families produce more harmonious families. Sadly, disharmonious families produce families in their own image. To guarantee healthy families by existing and new techniques is the greatest challenge to contemporary psychiatry.

Contemporary child care theory emphasizes the importance of a continuous relationship with one object, preferably the mother. This is an extraordinary distortion of the true situation. A child is brought up in a discontinuous relationship with a number of objects or subjects, anomalies in the psychopathology of the child care experts drive the child into a caged-in, locked, embrace with his mother alone. The child gains from a number of relationships rather than from a single one. All the essential ingredients of caring are to be found in fathers, aunts, uncles, grandparents, foster parents, etc. *The capacity to relate does not depend upon gender role, legal status, mental status etc., but upon the relating experience of that person in his own preceding family.* All these people too may have demonstrated a capacity to relate. All have a capacity as nurturers. And neither nature nor child cares who is the nurturer as long as nurturing occurs. Nurturing, like any other device in nature, is a contrivance to a particular end. The end is the important thing.

Others, as well as parents, have the capacity to love. Loving is dependent on experiences in childhood that evoke the potential to love; others do not differ from parents here. Foster parents can love as parents can — limitlessly, in tepid doses or not at all. If there is a choice between natural and foster parents, the question is not who has the legal rights over the child, but who can care for him best.

Children need love. If some cannot love them, others must. If the handicaps of the parents or misfortune make loving care by them impossible, then others must do the loving.

When children lose loving care, some, by chance, are fortunate to receive substitute care. We must no longer leave it to chance, as present-day practices tend to do. Maria had escaped from a lack of love and was thrust back into deprivation. The basic misconception that claims that natural parenting alone can give loving care is wrong. Practices must be adjusted.

Remember Maria. Remember too that after her death a witness at the Court of Inquiry said (*The Times*, 21 November 1973) 'Mrs Kepple's blood tie with the girl influenced decisions. She could not be regarded in the same light as a potential foster mother.' That misconception was a death sentence.

Chapter 5

The Evil of
No-Separation

If it is held that the 'special feeling' between parent and child is ever-present and so unique as to be irreplaceable, it follows that children should never be parted from their parents and, if they are parted, they should be returned to their parents at the first opportunity. This view led to Maria's fateful return to her natural mother.

The above views are misconceptions. Parental love is usually, but not always, present. Loving care is not unique to natural parents and many other people have the same capacity for it. In those fortunately rare situations, where loving is deficient, separation in the interest of the child may be essential.

Regrettably, a tradition has been established which regards that separation should be avoided at all costs and a child's own home should be preferred to any other home whatever the circumstances. Once we disprove this misconception we open the door to procedures of enormous benefit to both parents and children. Furthermore, since psychic trauma in the early years is at the root of psychonosis (emotional disorder), the door is simultaneously opened to new therapeutic procedures that can bring immense benefit to the emotional health of people.

THE BASIC MISCONCEPTION

The lonely child cries. Its appeal, so strongly stamped by nature, stirs the heart. The child needs the security of empathy, of love. The appeal should be, and usually is, answered by the child's parents. But what if the parents cannot respond? Help the parents to respond, is the reasonable answer. But what if the parents, rarely, have no capacity to respond and cannot be given it? Some would argue that even so the quality of the natural parental care is so vital that any substitution can be damaging. The child's own home, it is argued, is better for him than any other home; separation of child from parent is never justified. Another point of view maintains that more important to a child than the parent is loving care. Denied love in his own home, in an uncommon instance, it should have love elsewhere. So the controversy is born — can separation of child from parent be justified?

The theme running through this chapter is that separation is not synonymous with deprivation. Once clarity emerges about these two words then the matter is easily resolved. Most of the confusion about 'separation' and 'deprivation' springs from the fact that the two words are used interchangeably and it would seem to be essential to have a clear definition of each.

Separation of child and parent, by common usage, means that the child is physically parted from its parents and has an existence independent of them. In separation, child and parent are apart.

Deprivation is a term which indicates that a loss is suffered and when applied to the child it usually denotes that the child is deprived of the necessary loving care for its emotional growth. In deprivation, the child has lost love. Thus, *deprivation can occur with the parent, or apart from the parent.*

Separation, then, involves a physical loss of the parent, but not necessarily of loving care. When Maria was parted from the natural mother, she did not lose love. Deprivation, on the other hand, involves the lack of loving care, but not necessarily of parents. Maria lacked love when she was with her mother. Thus, 'separation' and 'deprivation' are not synonymous terms. Separation, then, need not lead to lack of love. Whether it does or not depends on the situation in which the child is placed. If it is a situation of loving care it can be a great opportunity and be of immense benefit.

The commonest occurrence of deprivation is with non-separation, i.e. due to stressful situations at home between parents and children. Separation of children and parents may sometimes be the best way of avoiding deprivation. However, the common view is that separation is the danger and that it is responsible for mental ill-health in children.

Contemporary expert opinion is often rigidly opposed to child–parent separation under any circumstances. Here the extent of the misconception in contemporary practice will be reviewed. Then the history of the misconception will be outlined. Subsequently the findings of one of the few direct studies on the issue will be described.

To give point to the discussion the findings of an ethological study will be presented. Finally, the implication of these studies from our point of view will be summarized.

THE EXTENT OF THE MISCONCEPTION

In the clinical field, it has always been evident that most children who are deprived of proper care are so deprived by being in a condition of non-separation, while living with their parents — deprivation reflects the relationship between themselves and their parents. However, the misconception has grown that emotional ill-health in children results not through parental inadequacy, but through separation. Thus separation is assumed to be a dangerous operation for the child, to be avoided at all costs. The child's own home is reputed to be better for him than any other home. To review the whole literature on this topic would be too lengthy, and therefore a few sample statements are taken at random to show how widespread is this misconception.

The following statements reflect the view of the informed public. 'How seriously and lastingly young children may suffer if separated for even a day or two from their mothers . . . has been abundantly proved' (*The Observer*, 15 February, 1959). 'As many parents know only too well the effects on a small child of separation from its mother can persist for a very long time' (*The Sunday Times*, 15 September, 1968). 'It is increasingly realised that mother–child separation may be harmful to young children even if separation lasts only for a few days' (*Pulse*, 21 August, 1971).

Expert opinion from respected authorities is often slanted in the same direction: 'On the truely psychological side there is evidence that separation from the parent or parent substitute before the age of 5 may have a serious effect on the emotional growth of children and may form the basis of neurotic reactions in later life.' *The Part of the Family Doctor in the Mental Health Service*, 1961, London; Ministry of Health. 'Bowlby's work needs to be taken seriously because of his immense contribution to medical and popular understanding of the harm done to little children by separation from their mothers, harm that is liable to lead to a permanent distortion of the personality and character' (Winnicott, D. W. (1962). *Br. med. J.* 1, 305). 'If there is a break between the mother and child in the neonatal child of about a month or more, this commences deliquency in later life' (Rendle-Short, T. J. *Medical News*, 13 June 1969). Heading in *Medical Tribune* (16 October, 1969): ' "Separation from a parent plays a major role in the aetiology of psychiatric illness" according to Dr. J. Bowlby, Director of the Tavistock Clinic's Department for children and adults'. 'Mothers who leave their children in day nurseries and factory crêches may be causing them irrepairable mental damage, a Swiss doctor told the International Conference at the Royal Society of Health in Douglas, Isle of Man yesterday' (*The Daily Telegraph,* 7 September, 1972).

Although this viewpoint was found to be fallacious nearly 20 years ago in the direct study to be mentioned later, the reverse viewpoint has been slow to exert itself. From time to time there has been a sharp comment from a judge. For example, 'Jailing a miner for three years for a baby's manslaughter, the judge said "It was a thousand pities that the child did not remain in the care of the local authority" ' (*The Daily Telegraph,* 19 May, 1972). Again, it was reported in *The Guardian* (16 January, 1970) that a mother wished to place her infant in the care of the local authority, as she felt unable to care for the child. The plea was rejected because of the 'likely effect of parting the child from the mother'. The child died. The Coroner commented 'I cannot see the point of leaving a child with its mother merely to let it die of starvation.'

Dr. Mia Kellmer Pringle, Director, National Children's Bureau agrees with the judge: 'A child's ties with his natural family were so overvalued that he was sometimes allowed to remain with parents who were clearly disturbed or who rejected him' (*The Daily Telegraph,* 23 September, 1972).

THE HISTORY OF THE MISCONCEPTION

The basis of the misconception lies long back in psychoanalytical theory and its stress on the importance of an unique continuous relationship with a mother figure in the early years. Once the uniqueness of the mother—child relationship was uncritically accepted and the evidence of a discontinuous relationship with a number of figures in the family ignored, writers found the way to interpret clinical work and research studies in the light of the misconceptions.

For instance, some clinicians discovered that in the histories of their patients could be found a history of separation from the mother. This history of separation was assumed to have causal significance. Closer examination would have disclosed the fallacies. Firstly, when a child leaves his parents permanently it is invariably due to either severe neglect or break up of the family. Those factors in the home that led to neglect and to the break up of the family naturally damaged the child. A damaged child seen just after separation is assumed to have suffered from the separation, but the damage was done by the trauma prior to the separation. Secondly, if damaged or undamaged children, following the separation, are put in a traumatic situation, e.g. an unsuitable foster home or institution, further damage will occur. Here again the damage is put down to the separation, when it is caused by the situation following separation. The fallacy was compounded further since children placed in happy homes settled down, their damaged state was repaired and naturally they did not attend psychiatric clinics. Therefore the benefits of separation were not directly assessed. Had a group of psychologically healthy separated children been seen, it would have been obvious that the traumatic factor in the children seen at psychiatric clinics was not the separation itself, but the loss of loving care that resulted from it. Separation would not then have been confused with deprivation.

The fear of separation had other unfortunate consequences. Hard driven, a clinician might be forced to rescue a child from the family by separation. The child would then be placed in some therapeutic establishment for a short period of time, a few weeks or months, and then be returned to the family — for the trauma to continue and for the rescue operation to have been unavailing. Should the family have become a blissful place while the child was away, to return him to it would be desirable and proper. But, as we shall see later, homes are very difficult to change.

Another unhappy consequence was that the term 'separation anxiety' became a slogan emphasizing the dangers of separation. This led parents to suffer anxiety lest they cause damage to their children by the slightest separation. Ameliorating and socializing influences were denied to the children by well-meaning, but ill-informed parents.

Direct research studies on separation itself were rare; occasionally light would be thrown on the subject as a consequence of another study. But one direct study did compare the emotional state of children following a history of separation by being in a sanatorium. They were compared by questionnaire with a similar group of children who came from the same area and had not been in a sanatorium. The study, unfortunately, did not control a number of factors: whether any difference might be due to differences in the two groups before they went into the sanatorium; whether any differences were due to the sanatorium care itself rather than the separation; and whether there were differences in the two groups of children following the sanatorium period, e.g. the sanatorium children may have lost schooling. Within the validity of the study the workers found only a slight difference between the two groups — only on the teacher's report form on 5 items out of 28 was there a difference, i.e. on 23 out of 28 items there was no difference. The study failed to confirm that separation itself was a damaging agent.

In the meantime there were numerous studies on deprivation; these all pointed in the same direction — children denied loving care suffered ill effects and these were often responsible for psychonosis (emotional disorder) at the time and later. It did not matter where the child suffered the trauma — at home, at school, in institutions, in foster homes — the ill effect was the same. Unfortunately, as the terms 'separation' and 'deprivation' were confused (indeed the terms were often used interchangeably), it was assumed that the results of these studies also applied to separation. In fact the commonest place for denial of loving care was at home. Only 1 child in 200 is separated from home and lives in the care of the local authorities; 199 out of 200 children live at home. Here is where the massive deprivation occurs — at home, in conditions of non-separation. Such was the fear of 'separation anxiety' that the possible benefits of separation, properly undertaken, were rarely considered.

A DIRECT STUDY

Twenty years ago the misconceptions about separation so hampered preventive work at the Institute of Family Psychiatry, Ipswich, that the workers at the Institute embarked upon a direct study and its results were published in *The Lancet* in 1955. It decisively contradicted the supposed dangers of separation.

The investigation compared separation experiences in a random sample of emotionally sick children with similar experiences in a control group of school-children of average emotional health. The children of both groups were living at home and the separations were brought about by the normal happenings of everyday life. The clinic group was an unselected random group of emotionally ill children and will be referred to as the 'neurotic' group. Each group contained 37 children, and the two groups were made as similar as possible. The first five years were investigated since the protagonists of the danger of separation viewpoint regard this as the most vulnerable age-group.

The main investigation explored the incidence of separation experiences in the two groups. Should separation be responsible for mental ill health in children, then it would be expected that (1) there would be a high incidence of separation in the sick group and (2) the incidence would be significantly higher in the sick than in the healthy group.

Any separation lasting over 24 hours in a child of either group was recorded. The results were analysed in a number of ways but the most meaningful table for our purposes compared the number of separations of children from their mothers. The results are shown in Table 5. The separations entailed either the mother leaving the child, e.g. going to hospital at childbirth, or the child leaving the mother, e.g. a holiday with grandparents.

TABLE 5

Number of Separations of Children from their Mothers

	Under 1 year		Under 2 years		Under 5 years	
	Control group	Neurotic group	Control group	Neurotic group	Control group	Neurotic group
Over 1 day	2	4	18	23	71	69
Over 3 days	2	3	18	19	59	53
Over 7 days	2	3	17	15	49	46

A number of conclusions can be drawn from this table:

(1) In both neurotic and healthy children the number of separations under the age of one year was very low. Only 5 children out of 74 had been separated for more than seven days. There was no significant difference between the groups. In the neurotic group only 3 children had been separated for more than seven days. It is said that separation under one year is highly damaging to children and accounts for later emotional ill-health. It is clear that separation is not responsible for the emotional damage in the neurotic group of children here as 34 out of the 37 had not experienced it in the first year and there was no significant difference from the control group.

(2) From another table it was shown that about a third of the children in both groups under the age of two have been separated from their mothers for more than seven days making 17 separations in the control group and 15 in the neurotic group. This indicates that in only a third of the neurotic group could separation from the mother at this early age have caused the neurosis; and this possibility is ruled out as no more occasions of separation occurred in the neurotic group than in the control group.

(3) By the age of 5 the number of separations in both groups was still low and there was no difference between them. We can draw the same conclusions as in (1) and (2).

From another table (Table 6) it was seen that the number of separations from father in both groups, while still low, was greater than from mother. This was found to be largely due to an obvious cause — fathers were away from home due to reasons of employment. No-one has suggested that these separations are significant in the development of emotional ill-health in children.

TABLE 6

Number of Children Separated from their Fathers

	Under 1 year		Under 2 years		Under 5 years	
	Control group	Neurotic group	Control group	Neurotic group	Control group	Neurotic group
Over 1 day	5	10	14	19	30	29
Over 3 days	5	8	14	17	28	26
Over 7 days	4	7	13	15	25	24

As the separation experiences were the same in the two groups some factor other than separation must be responsible for the disturbances of the neurotic group. From other parts of the investigation there was much to suggest that the quality of parental care was lower in the neurotic than the control group, i.e. deprivation or poor loving care was responsible. For instance, taking the mothers, it was found in the neurotic group that they had a greater incidence of illness — and illness is correlated with disturbance in adults. The mothers of the neurotic group of children rarely visited their children if they were admitted to hospital. That inadequate care was responsible was suggested by another part of the study. Two groups of children who had been separated from their parents but who had gone to different places, one group to hospital and the other group to non-hospital separation, care by a relative, were compared. The comparison showed much more temporary disturbance in the hospital than the non-hospital group making clear that it is the deprivation consequent on separation that is damaging and not the separation itself — most children were happy with their relatives. Out of 66 comments on non-hospital separation only 18 were unfavourable.

It is of immense importance to separate the circumstances surrounding a separation from the fact of separation, e.g. a mother might say 'My little girl has never been the same since I left her for four days.' She does not evaluate the whole experience and forgets that the four days' separation was due to her going to hospital for her second pregnancy from which she came home with an adored baby boy. Obviously, the little girl's life has never been the same since the advent of baby brother — the change was not caused by the separation itself.

The investigation threw light on the causes of children being parted from their parents, whether by the parents leaving the child or the child the parents. Mother's commonest cause for leaving the child was illness. Father's commonest cause was work. The child's commonest cause was his own illness or his mother's illness making it necessary for him to leave home. Of great fascination was to see how sensible parents were in managing the care of the child when mother was away. As can be seen from Table 7 they did the obvious thing; they left the child with

TABLE 7

Care of Child when Mother Away

	Control group	Neurotic group	Total
Grandparents	14	15	29
Other relatives	10	8	18
Friends or neighbours	3	8	11
Father with either siblings, relative or home help	13	9	22
Residential nursery or home	0	4	4

someone he knew and who could care for him, i.e. they prevented deprivation. Rarely did they seek residential care for the child.

When separations lead to loss of loving care, as can happen in hospital, the investigation showed that the child could be upset — but this was temporary as the separations wery usually brief. There was also much to suggest that happy secure children responded far better to being left. An upset, however brief, should be avoided. Parents normally do this when they can control the circumstances and place the child with relatives etc. But they have no control over institutions. Upset can be reduced by preparation of the child, calmness by the parent, a happy environment during the parting, visits by parents, visits by others known to the child and individual care.

'Separation anxiety' has unfortunately made parents cling to their children and the children in consequence are rarely parted from them. This makes it much harder for the child when he has to be parted, and especially if the parent is so guilty as to be anxious. Separations are not

harmful unless they lead to loss of love. Most separations do not, and
the child not only benefits from care by another loving person but also
learns to trust the adults around him, so that when separation is
inevitable, e.g. due to illness, he can trust Mummy and Daddy to visit
and knows that other people can be as nice as Mummy and Daddy. We
have to make sure that our hospitals and institutions are full of such
people.

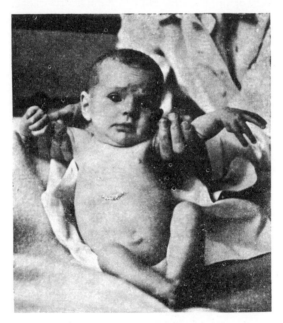

*Figure 8 – (a) The results of deprivation in the child's
own home (cont.)*

To conclude, the findings of the direct study were that the incidence
of separation in the two groups were very similar, and differences were
minor. Thus it could be concluded that separation does not, in most
cases, lead to emotional ill-health. The findings suggested that most
disturbed children suffered emotionally from being with their parents,
i.e. deprivation springs most commonly from inadequate parental care,
thus confirming clinical experience. The findings also showed that the
conditions applying before, during and after the separation are more

important than the fact of separation in determining whether or not
there will be harmful effects.

Furthermore, it appeared from the research that some children
actually benefited from separation.

The results of the study were so emphatic in making clear that

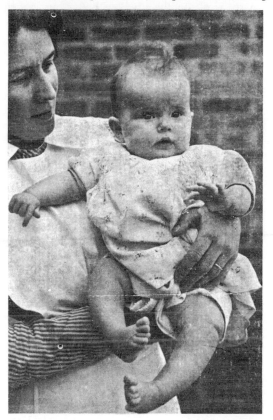

*Figure 8 – (cont.) (b) Very obvious improvement after
separation from the home*

separation need not lead to deprivation, that it became possible to use
separation procedures in a therapeutic way.

Some readers may wish for more details of the study and these can
conveniently be found, together with an up-to-date discussion of
related matters, in a Chapter by the same author in *Modern Perspectives
in International Child Psychiatry,* published by Oliver and Boyd.

OF MONKEYS AND MEN

There is merit in looking at this issue in detachment. An excursion into animal studies provides just such an opportunity and supports the findings that the damaging agent is deprivation and not separation.

Harlow's early work on the monkey behaviour is well known. Its recent extension has great relevance to our discourse, as a brief sketch will show. In the first part of their work Harlow and his colleagues were able to produce neurotic infant monkeys by deprivation consequent on separation. The infants were separated from their parents and became neurotic. The workers, mistakenly, thought that this was the result of separation. However, had the monkeys been placed with foster parents following separation, then the neurosis would not have appeared, i.e. separation would not have led to deprivation. It was not separation *per se* that did the damage, but the fact that it led to deprivation. The truth of this emerges again in a moment.

In the second stage of their experiments, the neurotic infants were allowed to become adults, were mated, and these disturbed mothers produced neurotic infants. These infants became neurotic because they were rejected by the mother, i.e. they were not separated, but they were deprived. The deprivation did the damage. (Similarly, a battered child is not separated from his family, but he still receives gross deprivation.) Then there was a dramatic intervention. The monkeys had to be rescued to prevent deprivation continuing to the point of death. And what was the intervention? The employment of separation! The infants were taken away from the depriving mother monkeys and placed with non-depriving adult humans. Separation was employed therapeutically to prevent deprivation and death. (Might not the battered child merit the same rescue?). The first two stages of the work confirm that separation is not synonymous with deprivation. Deprivation is the noxious agent. Deprivation can occur with non-separation to the point of death. Separation saved the life of the infant monkeys.

In the third stage of their work, Harlow and his colleagues were looking for a therapist for the disturbed neurotic infants. Behaviour therapy was tried, but was not effective. So stable, young monkeys were employed as companions to the neurotic monkeys, i.e. the depriving negative parents were replaced by positive non-depriving young monkeys. The negative forces were replaced by positive forces. The neurotic monkeys improved. (I mention this piece of research work because it has lessons for us in the treatment of emotional illness produced by damage in the home.) The young monkey had no knowledge of psychiatry and yet achieved improvement in his fellow monkey. If we understood what went on between these two monkeys with exactitude, we could plan precise procedures for psychotherapy by interview. But we are a long way from precision. However, we do know that the process of contact with a benevolent source works in the case of the monkey. Thus for the human there is another way as effective as psychotherapy — vector therapy. A vector is a force. The aim of vector therapy is to put someone through a process of contact with a healing force. Had Maria been returned to her foster parents, she would have improved with certainty. The damaging force from the mother would have been replaced by a healing force from the foster parents. We will return to this idea in the theme of treatment later in the book.

IMPLICATIONS

Maria Colwell underwent two separations. The first took her away from her natural mother and brought her benefit. The second took her away from her foster parents and brought her deprivation, loss of loving care, and led to her death. Her experience alone would show that it is not the separation that is dangerous, but the lack of loving care, i.e. deprivation.

The material collected here supports the above view. It makes it clear also that the commonest causes of lack of loving care are present in the child's home. Even though most families are happy, a substantial minority are not. The number of unhappy homes and unhappy children at home far outnumber the number of unhappy institutions and unhappy children in institutions.

Chapter 6

Recapitulation

Maria Colwell was returned to her natural mother because of the supposed everpresent loving care in a natural parent. The principles on which the decision was made were fallacious.

It was assumed in Maria's case that the loving care offered by substitute parents — her foster parents — could not match the unique loving care of her mother. That view is fallacious.

Maria was separated on two occasions. The first took her away from lack of adequate loving to the loving care of her foster parents. The second took her away from the loving care of her foster parents and put her in the inadequate care of her natural mother — inadequate to the point of death. As we have seen, it is not separation which is dangerous, but lack of loving care. Separation can sometimes lead to loving care.

Three further issues remain to be discussed. First, what are the conditions that cause families to be unable to supply loving care to their children. This is the subject of the next chapter — *The Vicious Spiral.*

Secondly, it is possible to intervene in the vicious spiral, and this is the topic of *The Quest for Health.* The book ends with a third issue, the means by which we can adjust child care practices, hence *Towards the Right Care.*

Chapter 7

The Vicious Spiral

Maria was born into neglect, escaped from it and was returned to it. Why does a home, a family, neglect a child?

The insightful Dr. Samuel Johnson *(Lives of the Poets)*, discussing the misfortune of the poet Savage, put it exactly: 'It is too common for those who have unjustly suffered pain, to inflict it likewise in their turn with the same injustice, and to imagine that they have a right to treat others as they have themselves been treated'. He could discern the vicious spiral. What a terrible mother Savage had! And what a terrible father he would have made.

We must always seek the answer one generation back. The parents of the present family were neglected in the preceding family, in their childhood. The fruits of the present neglect of the child will be seen one generation hence. The Marias of today, unless good fortune intervenes, become the neglecting parents of tomorrow. So we find neglect, deprivation, and incapacity for loving care passing from the preceding family to the present family and from it to the future family — a vicious spiral.

Over many generations, by chance, some ameliorating factors may appear, and the generations improve. Or over many generations, by chance, may come adverse factors, and the generations worsen. In the next chapter we will see that we do not need to leave this process to chance; we can intervene. In this chapter we must understand the process so that we can intervene with knowledge; the views expressed here are a digest of a wider exposition in *Principles of Family Psychiatry* by the same author.

TO BECOME SICK IN SPIRIT

To understand how sick situations cause a spiral of sickness, we have to enter the world of the psychiatrist (healer of the psyche) and the sick situations with which he is concerned — psychopathology (disease of the psyche, or of the emotions). At once it is essential to understand that we are not here discussing mental illness or insanity, but an entirely different condition — an illness of the psyche, emotional illness. Some would disagree with me and link mental and emotional illness. But my viewpoint is perfectly logical. Insanity, e.g. *true* states of the schizophrenia, is in some ways similar to delirium which is caused by physical agents, e.g. high fever or an overdose of certain drugs. Emotional illness is the result, not of physical agents, but of hurtful thoughts conveyed from one person to others. We all think of ourselves in a particular way. Indeed the most precious part of ourselves is the final idea we have of our own value. If we have no value, if we feel that we are worthless, then let us die. This idea of ourselves is the core of us. And it can be hurt. It can be hurt by attitudes communicated to us by others.

The more hurtful the attitudes the more we are damaged. The more vulnerable we are to particular attitudes the more we are damaged by them. The younger we are the more vulnerable we are, because we have not yet developed ideas that can protect ourselves. Naturally, we try to cope with hurtful ideas thrust at us. In fact we are usually very strong in this respect and adjust to a great deal of hurt. When the adjustment breaks down we show signs of damage and it is striking how these signs are seen in the body as well as in the spirit. An unhappy child looks unhappy and, when we ask ourselves what an unhappy child looks like, we will notice on close observation that he has actually changed physically — pale skin, lifeless muscles of the face, slower in movement, no gloss to his hair, low voiced, and shrunken.

What are these hurtful attitudes? They are all too familiar and some are very obvious — 'I hate you', 'Did you have to be born', 'Failed again, never as good as your brother'; and so forth.

Some hurtful ideas are devastating. Imagine a husband and wife together after physical intercourse. On the wife commenting that the husband did not seem to have fulfilled himself, he replies 'I was keeping that for someone else'. One can expect her to be hurt, angry, distressed, if not to vomit — certainly to refuse him intercourse, perhaps for ever. In contrast to hurtful ideas there are those that bring pleasure. Imagine the arrival of a new suite. The husband says 'I shall always sit on this settee'. 'And why?' says the wife. 'Because I can then always sit close to you' is the reply. The wife would be filled with pleasure and be radiant with the joy of it; body and mind are aglow.

Actions as well as words can convey hurtful, noxious ideas — to avoid someone in the street, to smile with disdain, to make a mocking gesture, etc. Some actions hurt by being negative rather than positive, e.g. not to send a card at someone's birthday but to remember everyone else's. Many people who are anxious, timid and fearful about sexual matters can never say that their families positively did anything to give them misinformation; it was just that whenever a sexual topic came up spontaneously there was a silence which carried an implication that this whole subject was unwholesome and taboo. We must take account not only of what is said and done, but also of what is not said and not done. Dylan Thomas put it very well in *Under Milk Wood*. The women were gabbling at the pump. Polly Garter, 'the lover and mother of all men', came by and 'You can tell by the noise of the hush'. Thus all the time the individual is beset by these attitudes continually being conveyed to him — some to his advantage, some to his disadvantage.

Where do these ideas, these meanings, come from? Naturally, as they are psychic, they have come from a psychic source — another person. Objects cannot hurt the psyche unless they convey an adverse meaning, e.g. a rather dilapidated house would not of itself hurt one's feelings, as some people are very happy with simple possessions, but it could hurt very much if it caused one's family to imply that because one has a poor house one is inferior. Hurtful ideas then come from people. In the early years the only people around the child are his family. These are the most important years because the child's vulnerability is so great.

It is just possible that, as a matter of fact, the first year or so may be less hurtful than later. The brain, the servant of the mind, is not very well developed at that time — perhaps to protect us from the trauma of birth — or putting it another way, we have to be born before the brain is well developed. Early on in childhood our memory is not well developed and maybe we forget happenings very quickly as well as having difficulty in taking in their meaning. The remaining years of childhood, it seems, are very impressionable.

The impressions, for good or evil, come from the other family members — father, mother, brothers, sisters, and any other intimates such as a nanny or grandmother in the family. Later, from 5 to 15, impressions begin to come from school, friends and others outside the home. But the family members are still very important. Even when at school a child still spends two thirds of his waking life at home. Not only does he still have much contact with his fellow family members, but when he is with them, the ideas they express are usually the same as those they conveyed in the past and meaning keeps accumulating with time.

The span of time is important. The main suffering of a little girl is not caused by father spanking her on a particular day — but by the fact that she has to live with the sort of father who spanks his little daughter. He might ignore her most of the time, and that hurts too, as it makes her feel that she is not even worth a little attention. Indeed one might prefer a spanking to being ignored, if it means to be recognized. We are brought up in families. In families are the people that we relate with in our tender years, our vulnerable years. Hence the immense significance of the family. Had we been brought up by the whole village, as indeed happens in some cultures, we could be understood only by understanding the village and the village would be the significant child rearing unit.

The individual who lives in his family is beset by converging attitudes from other members of the family — a whole pattern of attitudes. The pattern fluctuates from moment to moment. One moment it is for him, the next against, and then for him again. Most patterns in the family are in favour of children, even though they may fluctuate a little. Also the child can change the pattern to some extent. He can, for instance, move nearer those members of the family who are for him; a good reason for not ordaining that he should be brought up by one person only. Again, a discerning person can change the pattern by moving nearer the child. Or those professionally charged with his care can change the pattern by an intervention. This latter approach will be of concern to us later when we discuss vector therapy. The idea of vector therapy is to change this pattern of emotional forces that converge on people so that they are advantageous to them. The pattern of forces converging on the person may, on the other hand, be always to his disadvantage. Nobody can stand up to adverse forces for a long period of time without showing signs of damage. The family's pattern makes or breaks us. It makes most people. It breaks about a tenth of us and seriously damages about a third.

When hurtful ideas of great intensity, e.g. 'you hurt your mother, you just about killed her', or a string of hurtful ideas over a long period of time hurt the mind of the person at the receiving end, the mind tries to cope. It may say 'that statement is false, in truth I can say I did not hurt my mother and I know that my sister exaggerates'. This is a sensible appeal to reason and it can help — indeed nullify the hurtful idea. This is one example of a healthy way of coping. Another is the powerful mechanism of forgetting. We suffer the blow of bereavement — are numbed, then disturbed, and then the hurt recedes with forgetting and we remember only the pleasure that persons we have lost gave us. Sometimes we are not allowed to forget and one of the culprits can be

ill-advised psychotherapy − dragging up the past for the sake of dragging it up, and doing nothing constructive with the memories. Another
coping device is to deny that something was ever said, or believed in;
e.g. very rapidly the misconceptions outlined here will be denied, they
were never central in policy, never dictated action, it was all a rare,
unlikely, muddle, that will never occur again − though Maria died.
Hence the public reaction to forestall this.

Another common way of coping is to attack, 'You, my sister, killed
my mother'. This usually sets going a hurtful exchange which ends in
both people being bruised. Side issues are dragged in, 'Don't you
remember when you did the same to Aunt Nellie'? etc. Some try to
cope in phantasy − they build up a notion of themselves which is
highly moral − 'I am so good that I never hurt anyone' − despite
obvious contradictions in practice. When hurt, it is possible that the
mind keeps itself in a state of expectation, ever on the alert, lest hurt
comes − what is termed anxiety or tension; it even interferes with
sleep, as one must be perpetually on guard.

Normally the ways we attempt to cope − and there are many − are
taught us in childhood. For instance, if refusing to eat causes alarm in
the family, then one refuses to eat when one needs to retaliate against
the family. Later in life the same mechanisms are used as they have
become habit.

Again, the attitudes to which one is specially vulnerable spring from
childhood. There is a thunderstorm and the mother dives under the
bed. The idea conveyed to the child is 'thunderstorms are dangerous'. If
this idea is repeated a few times, even in later life thunderstorms will be
avoided. The opposite could happen in another family, where mother
takes her child to the window to see the beautiful lightning and to
wonder at the power of the universe. In the future, the child will react
to a thunderstorm with pleasure and wonderment. Unfortunately, ideas
conveyed with great release of emotion have a greater effect than those
inculcated with calmness. In the former, the idea of the self is under
attack and therefore everything to do with it is alerted and gets priority
even in the processes of memory.

It will be clear from the above that these ways of coping are passed
down the generations. A mother who fears thunderstorms will convey it
to her daughter, who in turn conveys it to the granddaughter. It will
pass down the chain of families, by word and not through the blood,
until something intervenes. In one family in the chain, a father who
happens to be closest to the child and who has no fear of thunderstorms conveys a new idea to the child − and the chain is broken. On
the other hand, if a wife and a husband who are both fearful of thunderstorms get together, the tendency to such a fear is accentuated. We will
see later how not only coping devices and special sensitivities are passed

down the generations, but so also are the signs and the symptoms that indicate the damage to the self.

When a little dirt gets into the petrol of a car, there is some temporary damage to the engine. It become less efficient, and power falls. The process of damage is right inside in the cylinders. We cannot see the damage, but we can guess at what is going on if we are knowledgeable enough. People, naturally, cannot be expected to know exactly the process of damage in themselves. In the case of the car, the driver is aware that something is wrong, as the car has backfired, will not take the hill, and is 'pinking'. An individual is aware that something is wrong with himself because he cannot sleep, has a rash and feels miserable. The driver tries to cope with his car – perhaps by pressing hard on the accelerator; if he is successful the gush of petrol will loosen the dirt and all is well; if not, the signs of dysfunction in the engine get worse, the car may even stop and the driver seeks the expert help of a mechanic. Similarly, the individual tries to cope at first, but when it becomes obvious to him, or someone else to him, that something is wrong which he cannot put right by himself, he seeks help.

What are the indicators that he has been damaged? There are two types of indicators – emotional and physical. On the emotional side he feels anxious, tense, miserable, irritable, angry, 'nervy', 'highly strung', guilty, unable to concentrate, depressed, and sometimes so anguished and worthless that it does not seem worth living. On the physical side he may fail to sleep, have headaches, stomach pains, loose bowels, develop a rash, his movements become jerky; in a woman periods may become heavy or cease. Every system of the body can be affected. Some of the physical symptoms are severe – a stomach ulcer can perforate, blood in the vessels of the heart can clot (coronary thrombosis), blood in the vessels of the brain can clot (cerebral thrombosis). Our emotions can and do kill us.

For too long emotional disorder (psychonosis) has been taken too lightly. It is a killer. It kills not only by making us feel so anguished that we prefer to die (in the United Kingdom, each year, at least 30,000 people attempt suicide), but it kills by causing severe physical illnesses, a few of which I have mentioned. It kills also by a steady lowering of the working of the body – people simply pine away. It kills too by making people who are physically ill disinclined to live – they die whatever is done for them. Lastly, they kill by making people irresponsible, and irresponsible people take risks, unnecessary risks; they become 'accident prone', e.g. many people rush through fog each year when they cannot see, and kill themselves.

That emotional damage plays such havoc on the body poses considerable problems for the doctor. He has to establish that it is an emotional and not a physical cause that did the damage. We can be breathless because we are frightened, but we can also be breathless if we have cancer of the chest. We can lack concentration if we are depressed, but we can also lack concentration if we have a brain tumour. We can

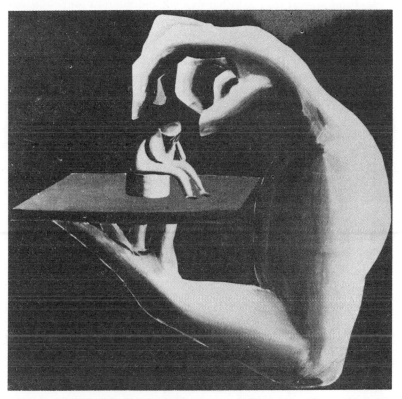

Figure 9 – Disturbed family; an adolescent's symbolic representation of his family

be listless because there seems no point in living, but we can also be listless because we have severe anaemia. Thus to find out what is wrong calls for considerable skill, training, and experience. To add to the doctor's difficulties, a patient can have a physical and an emotional illness at the same time — be depressed and have a tumour of the stomach. Just to make it even more difficult, there are times when a real physical illness creates a secondary emotional reaction — an engine driver who develops a cataract may have to change jobs and the uncertainty makes him feel depressed. In the profession a doctor gets his renown for his diagnostic opinion. It is these complex and varied states that test a man. This is why 'the opinion' is so highly valued, because given the wrong opinion, the wrong diagnosis, the treatment is bound to be of no avail.

Medicine, for as long as it has existed, and that is a long time, has been aware of this interchange between body and mind. Medicine is concerned with morbid states, dysfunction, illness (literally, to be 'ill at ease') of body and mind. Hippocrates, Avicenna, Galen and the physicians of the early civilizations were very clear about it – even back to the witch doctors. Right up to the Elizabethan period they treated 'the whole man'. A colleague and I studied a number of case histories left behind by John Hall, the physician son-in-law of Shakespeare, to find out how often he diagnosed emotional illness; he did so in about 30 per cent of his cases, just as our best physicians do today. Shakespeare was very clear about emotional illness – probably his knowledge was gained from Timothy Bright, who wrote the first textbook of psychiatry in English *The Treatise of Melancholy,* in 1585; it is possible that Shakespeare had a hand in the work involved in publishing it, as he seems to know it so well. Hamlet is a case history in psychonosis (emotional illness). But it is in *Macbeth* that Shakespeare describes the morbid state of the mind:

> 'Can'st thou not minister to a mind diseased;
> Pluck from the memory a rooted sorrow;
> Raze out the written troubles of the brain;
> And with some sweet oblivious antidote,
> Cleanse the stuffed bosom of that perilous stuff
> Which weighs upon the heart?'
>
> *(Macbeth,* V.iii)

At about the time of Shakespeare's death, Harvey made his great discovery of the circulation of the blood. It was to prove of great benefit in itself but it also opened the way to a massive upsurge of interest in body function; aided by scientific development elsewhere, it revolutionized our knowledge of physical illness with immense benefit to mankind, but, as in the rest of science, the psychic part was largely overlooked. Psychic functioning is more complex and less tangible. We now witness the redressing of the balance – starting with physicians such as Prichard, Morel, Freud, Janet and others. Freud was emphatic about the importance of his subject; in his *A Short Account of Psychoanalysis* he stated that psychonalysis was 'as definite and delicate as that of any other specialized branch of medicine'. Some would claim that illness of the mind is only a half of illness (half of being ill at ease). The truth is that physical and emotional illnesses are indivisible. To make both into a whole is the task of medicine in this century.

It may be noticed that in the explanation of psychic disorder there has been no mention of symbolism. It has not been suggested that those given to smoking cigars rather than cigarettes are attempting to cope with problems concerning their sexual organs. It is a matter of protecting one's welfare by switching from cigarettes to cigars and reducing the risk of lung cancer. This latter approach to psychiatry is termed 'experiential psychopathology' — a fact is a fact and does not need interpretation or falsification. The truth of the experience that happened to people is all. The symbolic approach arose from the understandable ignorance in the early days. It was intriguing and fascinating to indulge in these intellectual exercises especially as their folly could not be corrected by an appeal to knowledge. These theories tended to attract the type of person who preferred intellectual exercises to the hazards of reality and, in particular, those who needed to dwell on sexual anxieties.

Mysticism is obscure and therefore dangerous. As it is not possible to understand easily obscure concepts and thus prove them wrong, it is assumed that they must be right. This preoccupation with the fanciful, unfortunately, had to be paid for — it alienated realists, especially physicians forced to be realists by the everpresent immediate demands of patients in distress. The phantasy was interesting but did not help. Patients need help.

THE SICK FAMILY

We are now nearer understanding why some families are unable to give satisfactory loving care to their members. Clashing ideas and home conflict come from two main sources — the past and the present (within and without the family). Each can be taken in turn.

It is crucial to accept that the family is an organism in its own right — it has a structure of its own (like an individual), it has paths of communication within itself (like an individual), it has characteristics of its own (like an individual), and, very importantly, it has a mind of its own. This latter is the collective group mind of the family and this mind can be sick in the same way as the mind of a person. Its sickness can be detected in the same way, but we do not need to go into that here. Whence its sickness? It comes from the past.

A family in the present is made by the fusion of two families in the past — the family of the husband and the family of the wife. Each spouse is a part of the family in which he or she was born and in all essentials each of them is like that family. It is like cutting a cake into a number of pieces. Each piece has all the basic ingredients of the whole cake. Similarly, members of families, who superficially are and look different from one another, are alike in basic qualities, as each of them has had to conform to the climate of the same family.

Now, each of two families sends it representative forth into the future — and they meet up, court, and marry. If there is accord between them, it is not because they as individuals are in accord, but because the families, whom they represent, are in accord. If there is discord, it is not because they are discordant, but because the families they come from were discordant. Each is a puppet dancing to the tune of his family. If they are in step, all is joy. If out of step, there is conflict. It is possible for two people from disturbed families to be in accord, if their weaknesses counterbalance one another. However, the more disturbed the preceding families, and hence their representatives, the more weaknesses there are to clash with one another.

When the clashes are acute one of two things happen: the family, thankfully, fragments; but how cruel were our divorce laws in often preventing this! People after a divorce can have a second chance to make better family units. Divorce, properly guided, strengthens families. It is no excuse to say 'we kept together for the sake of the children'. thus keeping those children in their sensitive early years is the worst possible emotional climate. Divorce, handled calmly, can allow children to have the blessing of contact with two new harmonious families. The other thing that can happen is that highly disturbed family members keep together and batter one another to greater sickness and to death. A family in such circumstances, unable to part because of anxiety, or fear of the world outside, or because of public or family pressure, cling together and destroy one another.

The family can be a seething, fearsome, destructive place. Some families have such a high sickness rate that it may kill family members, they have a high suicide rate, a high rate of delinquency, of business failure, of alcoholism. Alcoholism, for instance, often results from an attempt to cope by numbing the senses that record too much anguish. Drug addiction has a similar cause. How absurd to assume that our adolescents are all likely to become drug addicts! Of course they are not! Most of them are charming and delightful, too little praised. But one in teh of them is unhappy. A proportion of unhappy adolescents has always been with us — a situation unlikely to change for a time yet. If you want to know what they have to cope with, ask them. I will guarantee that in a few minutes each will describe you a home that you would rather not live in.

These seriously disturbed families, greatly discorded, sick in the extreme, are often termed problem or hard-core families. The key to their understanding lies in understanding their emotional state. Material measures make no difference to them. We have tried environmental manipulation for years. A psychiatric illness needs a psychiatric prescription. An adequate assessment of the emotional state must be followed by an adequate emotional prescription. And even then, when it is clear what kind of help they need, the best psychiatric sources are sometimes going to find it difficult to cure.

As we have seen, preceding families make present families. Clashes in the present are a clashing of families, not of individuals. The key to the understanding of the present families is the understanding of preceding families. As Winston Churchill used to say 'The farther back you look the farther forward you can see'. These findings are central in family psychiatry and sprang from its main tenet — that the family is an organism in its own right, and can be sick in its own right. A sick person is only an indicator of the real patient, the sick family.

The past, then, can bring trauma into the present; each family sends into the present its own vulnerabilities, its own coping devices, its own ideas, its own signs and symptoms, and its own flavour of psychonosis.

But clashes can occur from the present too. Within the family there are happenings. Children are born and each child has differing meanings to each parent. I remember being called out just after Christmas to a man whose life had just been saved in hospital following a serious attempt at suicide. (What a terrible time Christmas can be in some families!) He had reacted badly to his wife's pregnancy and had been ill most of the time. (Again an example that illness can be understood only by assessing what is going on in the whole family.) The baby arrived. Wife was joyful. Husband morose. He was one of those fathers who wheels the pram to the end of the garden, and somehow forgets to wheel it back again. Things came to a head at Christmas. His hidden jealousy of the child erupted — some men are their wife's oldest child. The wife's parents called to bring presents for the baby. The husband locked himself in the kitchen and there was no Christmas dinner or any other sign of celebrations that day. On the next day he attempted suicide. After his recovery, his decision was stark and clear — 'The baby goes or I go'. The meaning of the infant was very different for husband and wife.

At birth, each child has also a different meaning for the children already in the family. A little girl may be a joy to her father, who always wanted a girl in the image of his much loved wife, but she has a quite different meaning to her brother who, before her arrival, used to hold the stage and have all daddy's attention. These are just a few of many situations that can develop in families.

In addition to trauma, resulting from past events and strain arising within the family, there is another source of trouble, events outside the family. A man or a woman can be subjected to strain at work from fellow workers, or the child at school may be victimized by one of the other children. This trauma comes from people, of course, and not from objects. But in a disturbed family the trauma arises from within itself much more often than from outside. Indeed, outside events are often blamed in order to obscure, wittingly or unwittingly, events within the family.

THE GENERATIONS

Children, then, find themselves in the family, not a family of their choosing. Most children are fortunate. The family, in general and allowing for minor fluctuations and unavoidable mishaps, is a harmonious unit. We rightly revere the family. It is a soundly constructed unit of male and female. There is a strong biological tie between them. Men and women are naturally attracted to each other and this is good and wholesome. The family has male and female children of varying ages. It is supported by its preceding and collateral families. A number of people make different roles possible. The family is a unit small enough to be cohesive and have good intense interactions. But some children are not so fortunate. Anger and bitterness ebb and flow around them continually, hot wars are followed by cold wars. Adverse patterns of ideas develop around them. The patterns leave their mark — they must.

This damaged child of a damaging family now goes forth into time, and seeks a partner. By good fortune, it may find a completely compatible partner from a compatible family. But chances are heavily weighed against him — his disturbed family, through him, will do the selecting. And it is unlikely that his choice will be wise. Furthermore people who move in the shadows meet people who move in the shadows — and come together. So unless good fortune intervenes, the present sick family meets another and produces another. Hence our vicious spiral.

We can see how emotionally handicapped parents are produced. But what produces angry, punishing parents? The poet said it all 'Force from force will ever flow'. Some families indulge in harmless shouting, trying to the ears but meaning nothing. But some families shout to hurt, and hit to hurt. Conflicts are solved in this fashion. The child is brought up to regard aggression as the appropriate coping device. 'Shout him down or force him physically to shut up or do as he is told' is the message. Nobody teaches him this; it is in the behaviour of the family and he quite naturally imitates it. But why devalue others so that they are hurt or destroyed? I recall an instance related to me by a social worker. She had been visiting one of our problem families and was coming out of the door with the father, the little baby boy and the dog, a greyhound. Ahead lay a steep flight of steps. Father ignored the child who all but tumbled down the steps, but picked up the dog, descended the steps with him, carefully put him down and murmured 'Can't have him breaking his legs.'

In some families people are not valued as such. It is understandable enough. If one has been hurt a great deal by people one ceases to believe in them. Indeed things, or animals are safer. Lovely money never shouts or hurts one; indeed money can protect, as most things can be bought. Hurt people are unpredictable and demanding. One comes to feel that they are not important in the scheme of things. They deserve to be devalued. If they happen to look like a hateful father, how can one control one's feelings? A man said to me 'You know, I did not regard my father as a human being until I was an adolescent and met group-ups who didn't frighten you to death'. So aggression is manufactured and others, mattering little, become objects for destruction.

Before we leave the matter, let us reflect that any hate from us will not help the above situations. We must – absolutely must – go hard over in the opposite direction. There is only one antidote to hate, and that is love. We can reflect also that emotional problems do not respond to material or social actions. Delinquency or alcoholism or suicide are problems of society in that, like tuberculosis in years gone by, they are rife amongst people. Physical medical problems respond to the appropriate treatment, which, overtime, has been reached through research and effort. Equally, psychiatric problems will respond to appropriate treatments, when we have the resources to work them out. Once elucidated, both physical and psychiatric illnesses can be reduced by preventive programmes – but only if guided by the knowledge that comes from the elucidation of their pathology. On the psychiatric side we are way behind in our knowledge and resources, but things are moving.

IMPLICATIONS

What has been said in this chapter again supports the view that parents are not always loving, not possessed of loving qualities that others cannot possess, and that children need not, and should not, stay in their own families, to be irreparably damaged, in the small number where this occurs. If we had these precepts we can plan action on a realistic basis.

Families make families. Unhappy families make unhappy families – 'in their own way' as Tolstoy said. These unhappy families spiral into the future on their fateful course. We wish for no battered children battering in turn the children of the future. We wish for no emotionally ill children, far more common than the battered children, who in turn become the sick parents of the future. We wish for harmonious families that give a happy harmonious milieu to our Marias, who make the families of the future.

How we intervene in the vicious spiral is the topic for the next chapter.

Chapter 8

The Quest for Health

Maria Colwell should not have been returned to her natural home. This was the cardinal error. She should not have been returned to it because that home was too handicapped to care for her. In the last chapter we have seen how families become handicapped — the victims of events beyond their own control. In these families there is a severe degree of emotional illness and thus emotional deprivation. We now need to study what actions can be taken to help — not just the families of battered children, for they are a minority — but all such families, which represent about a third of all families.

Our challenge is the sick family, the product of preceding families, sick in the past. They flow by into the future to found more sick families. Let up grasp one as it goes by and see what we can do to change it.

There it is: a depressed, past-caring wife, an angry husband, tortured by his stomach pains, a rebellious boy with asthma and a little girl who whines and frets. The adults can truly agree about one thing only, they are unhappy and the forced marriage was a disaster to be tolerated 'for the sake of the children'. Tension mounts. Mother holds it off with longer periods isolated in bed. (I know an intelligent woman who, as the tension grew in the family, could not pass water; when her abdomen had swollen to its limits, she had to isolate herself in bed, away from the strain, for four days before she could pass water and get the swelling down.) Father, fond of his pint, drinks excessively to numb the anguish of living and becomes an 'alcoholic'. It does not help his stomach. The boy has to be kept at home as much to keep the mother company as to help his asthma. Indeed staying at home makes his asthma worse. The little girl finds comfort in food and is overweight with eating — 'sad fat'.

Families like the one above come for help. Who comes? Rarely the family as a whole, although with the increasing co-operation of the family doctor it now happens more often. Usually an individual comes. It might well be the husband who, unable to tolerate the pain of his stomach ulcer, goes to the family doctor for tablets. Or possibly the mother, in desperation, attempts to end it all and finds her way into a general medical ward for the 'wash out' that saves her life. The boy's absences are noted. The school is concerned. Is the asthma a story? To the school doctor to find out. Schools can play a very helpful part. It allows someone other than a parent a close contact that can lead to enquiry about the state of the child. If mobilized in treatment, schools can offer a compensatory milieu for the child. The little girl gets fatter and someone asks why. You notice how it is often a physical symptom which first demands attention. It is a more obvious and more respectable claim on help; its dangers are also more evident. At least a third of patients attending the family doctor's surgery (and he sees 80 per cent of his list of patients each year — a contact with the public nobody else can match) do so with emotional illness, but two thirds of them come back with physical complaints. Hence the need for medicine to go back to its stance of 400 years ago and practice a medicine of the 'whole man'. Thankfully, the family doctor is showing much promise of doing it. Easier, too, for the family doctor to treat physical and emotional conditions together; in hospitals there has to be specialization.

It may have occurred to you that each of the four members of this family might have gone to a different clinic — father with his ulcer, mother with her depression, the boy with his asthma and the girl with her overweight. But how wasteful it would be! Four clinics trying to solve one problem! For it is clear already that each of these four people is battering the other practically to death. You cannot understand one without understanding the other. In technical language that is a 'polydynamic system', i.e. any event in any part of it affects the rest of the system.

Hopefully, one of the clinics concerned sees the need to refer to a psychiatrist not just one person, but the whole family. Hopefully, the psychiatric clinic will see them as a family. The first step is assessment, diagnosis. Nothing must be done that will make the tensions greater, or we may lose a family member — father's ulcer may perforate or the mother make another serious suicidal attempt. The whole family must be watched, otherwise a part of it may be hurt or lost during treatment.

If only one member of the family comes, it is more difficult for the rest; he or she is strengthened by the visits and can hit all the harder, emotionally that is. The victim may not even be seen by the psychiatrist or he may hear only a vague reference to Willie's asthma, that is getting so bad that he is now in hospital.

Diagnosis will tell too whether a physical illness co-exists with the emotional disorder; one can be very depressed and have cancer at the same time. Diagnosis will decide how much physical treatment needs to be given, how it is to be handled, and who is to handle it. It will decide how ill the family is, emotionally and physically. It will decide whether anyone is mad; but madness is a rare event, unless one calls every emotional illness madness. If emotional illness is confused with *true* madness then, as emotional illness is curable, it can be claimed that madness has been cured, and this, in my experience is a delusion. Diagnosis will also decide what assets the family has — these assets will be used in treatment. Diagnosis, in short, must come before treatment.

Another step follows diagnosis. It has been decided that the family is sick, but we do not know why it is sick. Now comes a careful screening of the family under a systematic enquiry in all its dimensions. This is not a hit and miss affair any longer. It is as systematic as an examination of the body. Always, and this is a lesson we have already learnt earlier from experiential psychopathology, the preceding families must be screened too. We have learnt the lesson well. We can understand this family only if we understand the families they come from. Only then will all be revealed. Now we understand why this family behaves the way it does — the attitudes from the past that control it and why A must clash with B and B with C and why C supports A. They all dance to the tune, often fateful tune, composed by the past.

Having understood, we can help. Let us imagine we have ideal facilities. Three choices are open to us. The first is the therapy of the word — psychotherapy. The second is that we might repattern the set of forces playing within and without the family — vector therapy, mentioned before. The third is a programme of health promotion — make the whole society, and each family within it, emotionally healthy. The third approach, in the fullness of time, is more valuable than the second, and the second is more valuable than the first. But let us be realistic; the family may say that it cannot wait a few generations for help. The truth of the matter is that all three approaches are valuable. From the first comes some help, and something of an inestimable worth — knowledge. We could not have mass x-ray to screen for tuberculosis until the disease was recognized, its pathology understood and the tuberculosis bacillus isolated. The second, vector therapy, is the most valuable form of treatment with our present resources and it puts our money, as it were, where it can be spent best – on the future. The third approach, over the generations, will be the most rewarding; fed by knowledge from the first two it will allow of a repatterning of the forces within society and create a health promoting society, truly salutiferous.

Psychotherapy aims at the psyche of the family and effects a change in it by using the psyche of the psychiatrist. It takes time. A lot of time. The process that set up the disharmonies in the members of the disharmonious family took time to work. It takes time to undo it. And time is money and resources. The job can be done. I like to call the job 'benexperiential therapy', i.e. we must bring a benevolent experience to operate for a long period of time to counteract the noxious experience. There are two targets that can be set. The first is concerned with making each adult member of the family, and thus the children, completely whole in all circumstances. A mighty undertaking. The second is a large assignment too. We take those clashing parts of the two adult members of the family and ameliorate them. It brings harmony in the circumstances of that family – and that is probably all that matters to that family.

Much has been written about the technique and efficiency of this form of treatment. When one remembers the facile assumptions on which it is based – and some of them killed Maria Colwell – we can see that there is a long way to go to reach precision. Freud took psychotherapy seriously. He likened it to surgery, surgery of the mind. He would be astounded if he saw the army of enthusiastic 'surgeons' at work today. He would be appalled at the carnage. It is assumed that as long as someone of little experience, uncertain knowledge, and of indifferent personality, talks to someone else some good will be done. It can equally do harm. And most of it does just that. We are at a moment when we should restrict psychotherapy until the time when certain knowledge has developed and given our technique precision. Better no surgery than bad surgery. Increasing numbers of psychotherapists merely escalate the damage.

Perhaps I have been too severe in my strictures. Perhaps, only a little. There are people proceeding with great discretion and care, not attempting too much, garnering knowledge as they go. It is this knowledge which is the precious thing. Here we can learn of the basic mechanisms that dictate human behaviour. This is the fascination of psychiatry.

Psychotherapy, when precise, has one severe limitation – it takes time. If a father is an angry beater of children and it takes four years to get the man balanced, the children can suffer an awful lot of damage in that time, and at a time when damage matters. If a child's foot is put in a tight unyielding shoe for four years, that foot may be crippled for ever. Children cannot wait too long in the hope that their parents will become better mothers and fathers. Psychotherapy, as it takes time, naturally absorbs much manpower. Very few psychiatric clinics can give a family more than two hours a week. Happily there are shorter and better methods.

This takes us to vector therapy. Here the first need is an accurate emotional assessment. The family meets, and is understood, as a whole. After a time its strength and weaknesses emerge and the pattern of forces is clear. It becomes evident where the upsetting influences come from. Here is an example, shortened and simplified to bring the principle into relief. Father was sullen and impossible. Little Harry soiled himself every day. The little chap was in a state of perpetual fright. Now, father, and the man I am thinking of was severely handicapped, could have been given psychotherapy. It would have taken perhaps four years to balance him if a psychiatrist were available – a big if. But could Harry take this battering for another four years? His mother solved the problem for him. A very insightful woman, she organized vector therapy. She decided to reduce the appalling weight of forces playing on Harry from his dad. She persuaded him to go on night duty – overtime to save up for a car. Dad was less at home. When he was at home at the same time as Harry he was in bed. When they occasionally met, she always contrived to be there to counterbalance father's sullen anger. As much as it was reasonably possible, she would send the child to his uncle, her brother, who was good with children. She reduced the intensity and time over which dad's temper operated and replaced it with a helpful influence from an uncle and support from herself. Harry stopped soiling and became a happier boy. Dad could, for his own benefit, still have psychotherapy. But the boy is safe – we have spent less resources and we have put our money on the future. Harry represents the future.

You will have noticed also how separation was used here as a technique. Harry was separated as much as possible from his dad. The misconceptions we have been talking about would have kept Harry with his dad, if the influence of the natural parent were assumed to be always good and irreplaceable. The doctrine of no-separation would have nullified this programme.

There are many manoeuvres that can be employed to change the pattern of forces within and without a family. A programme was outlined by the author in *Family Psychiatry* in 1963. A number of manoeuvres do not employ separation, some do. We do not need separation to change roles within a family. A young mother is very distressed. Her child is disturbed. Her agitation and guilt grows as she

mismanages the child. Father stands by helplessly and goes fishing more
and more − one of the respites of the troubled. He is sorry, but he has
always been told that mothers bring up children. It is a bad business,
but not his business. A few interviews disburden him of this notion
gained from his family and gives him hope of being able to do things for
the boy. He takes on the main parenting role. He makes it his business to
get close to the boy and to interest himself in him every possible
moment; he takes him fishing. Improvement in the boy and relief for
the mother follows.

Naturally, this approach calls for facilities. A number are often
unavailable. Hundreds can be employed, but I will concentrate on those
effecting a change of patterning in pre-school children. Ameliorating
influences can come through a nanny in a higher income group (but
help is required in her selection; angry parents choose angry nannies).
In all income groups one can employ day foster care. Using the Child
Minders Act it is possible for children to go during the day to carefully
selected, warm and loving substitute parents. Puny children are seen to
gain weight and young mothers learn to relax and enjoy them when
they can be made to accept without guilt their limited parenting
capacity. Playgroups bring the care of one or more warm persons; the
public have themselves put the no-separation measure aside and gone
their own way to found thousands of groups in the United Kingdom.
Some of these groups can be informal − five mothers get together and
look after the children for one day. Five nice mothers. Or if one is not
so nice, there are still four nice ones. Then there is the day nursery for
groups of children needing special care − special emotional care. Then
the nursery school − special nursery schools with carefully selected
staff. For older children there are special day schools and classes for
vulnerable children. The schools for physically handicapped can now
help the emotionally handicapped too. Later on there are evening,
weekend and holiday special schools for the vulnerable.

The principle is clear. Adverse influences in the pattern surrounding
the child are replaced by benevolent influences. Without the child
leaving its home the community can make an immense difference to his
upbringing. Ameliorating influences surround and support the family.
The community takes a hand in nurturing its weaker families for its
own self improvement. As the demand for hospitals, prisons, and
institutions lessens, there can be an increased investment in the family
with a snowballing effect.

Sometimes, after careful assessment, separation procedures are
found to be necessary. John Clare, the so-called mad poet who was not
mad at all, told us the cause of his melancholy; he felt 'never at home at
home'. How Clare would have profited to have had some substitute for

his bleak home! Instead, having no friends to help him, he could make no friends:

> 'I am — yet what I am, none cares or knows;
> My friends forsake me like a memory lost:
> I am the self-consumer of my woes.'

We can take the Clares of this world and bring them up. And the parents will not mind if they and we can be honest about handicaps and they can help by giving their child a chance. It follows that we cannot as a society alienate handicapped families; we and they can only profit in friendly partnership. We must be clear that we cannot educate people out of an emotional illness; a pathological process responds only to a therapeutic process.

There are a number of separation procedures, e.g. partial separation in the form of hostels for emotionally deprived children and special boarding schools for similar children. A foster home might be preferable to a boarding school, but sometimes the latter is all that a family will accept. Children and adolescents who are too disturbed to be cared for in these ways require the highly specialized care of an in-patient unit — and then, after amelioration, they can be transferred to one of the other facilities.

When a family simply cannot be adjusted, either because of resistance, severe degree of illness, or lack of facilities, in a small number of cases permanent separation becomes urgent. Foster homes and adoptive homes come into their own. Nine times out of ten, with careful friendly work, the natural parents can be brought to see that fostering or adoption will improve the situation for them and for their children. Guilt naturally causes clinging. Lack of blame and honest acceptance of handicaps are the antidotes — together with praise for helping their child. In the hierarchy of desirable substitute homes, adoption is at the top, followed by fostering, cottage homes, hostels and boarding schools. In a given situation, one must practise the art of the possible.

The principle is to change the forces acting on the family — not the material, religious, social or educational forces, but the emotional forces. It calls for warm non-coercive contact with families, a discussion of the emotional climate, the pin-pointing of adverse influences, the outlining of targets and often their achievement by the use of the family's assets or the community's facilities. The queen of the community facilities is the admirable social worker. Virtually all these facilities are now together and can be used in a coherent concerted policy. Nevertheless we must be realistic and acknowledge the immense, obvious, and even mundane demands, made on a department of social service. It will take time to deploy new facilities into the emotional field.

There is immense hope in vector therapy. We do not even need to cure everyone. If we can effect in each generation a 10 per cent improvement rate, then over the generations this will snowball — a few generations hence will attain a level of emotional health undreamt of today.

We still have our third programme, a programme not for single families, but for all families. In society too there are many adverse influences impinging on groups and on families, influences that are adverse to emotional health. A large scale analysis of society's functioning would reveal many of these. It could be shown, for instance, that children of unplanned pregnancies are at greater risk of rejection than those of planned pregnancies. By a policy of birth control, leaving aside the more controversial policy of extending birth control into the first three months of pregnancy, it would be possible to reduce the number of unwanted children and thereby, inevitably, make a small but significant improvement in the level of emotional health.

Again, a policy of no divorce weakens the family as an institution. Dysfunctioning families have thereby to be kept whole and produce the weakness of dysfunctioning families in the future. Freer divorce would allow families to quietly fragment in peace and harmony and for the fragments to form better unions. Guidance is required over the new unions. In time, as the healthier units make healthier units, the divorce rate would drop.

Every practice, principle, law, institution could be examined in the light of the question 'does it promote sound emotional living?' Many elements in society would be found wanting — in some countries the police are too coercive and produce violence; schools can sometimes produce a cult of competitiveness which is extreme; hospitals produce anxiety in relation to sickness; we are not yet reconciled to the inevitability of death; prisons make more delinquents (though in mitigation it must be said that until there are alternative procedures they are forced to practice a custodian role); material prosperity is assumed to be the key to well being (a common delusion). And so we could go on. A massive reassessment of society is needed. It must be done with care after planned investigation; mistakes are easy to make as we grope for knowledge — remember the damage of the 'no-separation' slogan. But reassessment is possible, indeed essential. It could bring the opening of a golden era of greater bliss and content-ment, a promotion of emotional health, a salutiferous society.

Chapter 9

Towards the Right Care

The clinical programme outlined in the previous chapter is the final answer. It will in time eradicate emotional illness in children. It follows that it would solve the problem of the battered child.

Battered children, like Maria, are the visible and obvious sign of a far greater problem. Merely to prevent children being battered is simply to remove the most obvious symptom and leave the main condition untouched. To achieve a situation where there are no battered children by attention to this one manifestation alone could be even dangerous. Children might not be battered physically any more – but battered in other ways; they could be battered in ways that are less observable. If it were assumed that all was well, a mood of complacency could arise which would leave the far greater problem of emotional battering untouched. This is not to argue that nothing should be done to prevent children being battered. Of course measures should be taken to prevent it, but alone they are not enough.

Sir Keith Joseph, Secretary of State of Health and Social Services, has put it very clearly when he addressed the Samaritans (*The Daily Telegraph*, 16 September 1973): 'The hundreds of children who are battered to death each year by their parents are only the tip of the iceberg . . . tens of thousands more were battered, but not to death, and hundreds of thousands were battered emotionally by their parents.'

In any society, as yet, there is always a limit to resources. Any one generation can afford to invest only some of its resources on its own self improvement. Maria's case, I hope, has shown the need to build a large-scale programme for the emotional sustenance of families. But the aged, the mentally handicapped, the schools and many other deserving causes require resources. What we can do now is to acknowledge this need and establish it as a part of our total programme. We must fashion a long-term clinical programme, in conjunction with related fields, to ameliorate the total situation.

However, immediately, the case of Maria Colwell calls for a re-examination of the effectiveness of the whole field of child care — embracing various fields and professions. A number of matters will be discussed here. They are general and do not apply to the case of Maria Colwell alone. If professional matters are the subject of comment they are meant to refer to all the helping professions and not to any particular one.

Before selecting certain major topics for fuller comment it may be useful to outline some general principles:

(1)   However efficient an organization, if it is working on wrong concepts, it cannot achieve desirable targets. The misconceptions, the subject of comment in this book, were not held by one profession only but by a number of professions. If these professions persist in being guided by these same misconceptions, with greater dedication and more co-ordination, they will simply succeed in killing more children.

(2)   While time, much time, will be required to fulfil the total programme leading to emotional health, if we rethink the deployment of even our present resources more in emotional terms, much can be achieved *now* without a great drain of resources, e.g. legislation aimed at not removing our Marias from good foster homes will alone achieve a great deal. If we can go beyond this and see that sometimes the need to separate our Marias from very seriously damaging and handicapped homes, we can do even more. Again, if we could rid ourselves of the idea that everyone can be a happy loving parent, we would stop blaming those who cannot, and once we stop blaming, they will admit so much more readily the need for help. In other words a change of thinking will make a highly profitable start.

(3)   Whenever there is misgiving about some aspect of an organization there is invariably an appeal for more money and more staff. Very often all that this succeeds in doing is to obscure the failure and to leave it untouched. Fifty-six visits in just over a year were undertaken to Maria's natural home while she was in it. That is a considerable expenditure of resources. With the right concepts one visitor for twelve worthwhile visits would have been more effective. But resources are wasted by being scattered into numerous hasty visits by a variety of people.

(4)   It is tempting to seek a stop gap, a short-term policy, panic measures, and quieten things down and forget the need for a long-term steadily developing programme.

(5)   When things go wrong families tend to blame one of their members, thus making a scapegoat. Society can do the same. It could do it in Maria's case. But nobody in the helping professions wished her death. There was no ill intention. Imperfections will emerge and teach us lessons, which we should use constructively.

(6)   Children are important. So are parents, they were children once. Our children will soon be parents. Thus any programme must be aimed at helping all age groups. The meeting of age groups is in the family. The maker of new families is the family. In clinical work I find that if I accept an adult patient I spend much time discussing his childhood. If I accept a child patient I spend most of my time discussing with his parents. The only way out of this confusion is to have the family together. The family is the optimum unit in the fields covered by the helping professions.

Some matters now deserve rather fuller discussion.

RESPONSIBILITY

Society has many tasks towards its self improvement. No one specialist can manage them all. Each field has its own specialists, be these agriculturalists, lawyers, doctors, engineers or teachers. The deployment of the many welfare resources of the community has become, by common consent, a matter for the social worker. Sometimes, as the term 'social' is in her title, society has assumed that all and every diverse social task must be in her field. This is a misunderstanding that places an unfair burden on the welfare services.

In carrying out society's tasks, it is a weakness of our times that more emphasis is given to co-ordination and communication than to responsibility. It is assumed that if everyone co-operates all will be well – this is the vague, ill-defined panacea of good intention. 'Lack of communication' is the supreme mechanism for whitewashing failure. Carried to its extreme it will result in a large number of ignorant ineffectuals 'co-operating'. Nothing will happen, except inconsequential talk.

Committees, case conferences, teams, huddles also have become the face saver of our time. They all have vast deficits. They are time consuming, expensive, they operate at the speed of the dullest, slowest or most awkward, blur the distinction between the job of each expert, sometimes are nothing but a platform for status seeking, and make nonsense of confidentiality. The biggest weakness of these conferences is the way in which they obscure the source of responsibility.

Co-ordination is no substitute for responsibility. It is best to have an expert, out in the open, with a well defined role, and precise responsibility. Nothing sharpens expertise more than responsibility.

Co-operation is of course useful. By all means people should come together for quick rapid discussions at the interface of a problem. But this is secondary to responsibility. As it applies to the field of social work, the press release by the British Association of Social Workers is apposite (*Social Work Today,* 29 November 1973). It states '. . . it is the application and development of social work skills which offer the best chances of minimising child abuse and suffering.' They have it right.

Professional intervention will be efficient and effective if one person only is responsible for deploying the welfare services for a particular family. Behind the worker responsible for a family can stand a number of specialists in various aspects of the welfare services, available for consultation and support, but not immediately responsible, e.g. home help service, meals on wheels, day foster care programme, day nurseries, etc.

The emotional and physical health, as distinct from the welfare aspects of home care, must be a matter for the family doctor with the family health visitor and, of course, the immediate bedside care of district nurse and midwife. The health service also requires its background support of a large number of specialist services.

It will be of no help to blur the distinction between these two services. Indeed, it will improve co-operation to make distinction of role clear to all, for then each worker can be secure and efficient in his own field.

EXPERTISE

Expertise based on experience and training and the right selection of personnel is the fundamental commodity in effective action in the health professions. Within these strictures, the expert is the best person for the job. It becomes the expert's prime responsibility to make decisions. Naturally, misconceptions can weaken them, but it is the function of the profession concerned to establish right concepts — and not of the administration. Each professional, secure in his role, will consult other professionals from whom it is relevant to have information, to take concerted action, or to hand over a situation. But the initiative should come from that worker and the decision should remain with him. Vague role allocations lead to vague collective discussions and a situation where no-one can be held responsible. Decision making is avoided. This avoidance, however, is often a positive act, e.g. not to take the decision of removing a battered child from his home is a positive act, which has dire consequences for the child.

This is the moment to talk of the pyramid, one of the enemies of expertise. A hierarchical structure of organization, the pyramid, is unsuited to the helping professions. Able people, because of the pull of remuneration, status, or simply to avoid working under someone whom they regard as less competent than themselves, are pulled up the pyramid and away from the field of their expertise. Administration, of course, is an expert craft, but its status and rewards ought not to be higher, nor lower, than those of other experts. Unhappily, a profession often finds that those at the top of the pyramid become powerful in the councils of the country and their voice alone may be heard. A powerful professional body, representative of its experts, is the solution. It is refreshing to hear the British Association of Social Workers state in a press release that there is a need for the encouragement of social workers 'to stay in the field'.

Alongside expertise we must study optimum size of groups. In every organization there is an optimum number of people for whom one can be directly personally responsible. I will illustrate from the medical field, which I know best. In nursing it is a ward, in hospital administration it is a hospital, in geriatrics a group of patients. It is possible for one person to supervise a group of aids and know enough of what is going on to be personally responsible for the main decisions. Let us take the consultant physician as an example. He has a group of patients, who usually have severe, complicated and dangerous conditions. A number of junior doctors will work with him. But his group of patients is small enough for him to be personally responsible for each. The health service is built round the concept that every patient has consultant care. The consultant may not give the blood transfusion himself, but he knows it has been given. The average consultant is appointed at the age of 36, after eighteen years of training since leaving school, and the expertise gained from this is available to each patient. This is the strength of the National Health Service.

The pyramid can destroy expertise, not only by pulling the expert away from his job, but by making the group too large. In all professions, experts should be kept in personal charge of optimum groups. This can happen only if rewards higher up are not so great as to pull the best people up the pyramid. It should not be worthwhile, either in money or status, for anyone in the health professions to go into administration, unless he has a flair for it and finds job satisfaction in it. The pyramid should be flattened. In the welfare field there must be an expert of considerable training close enough to families to be able to make immediate personal decisions.

For expertise to flourish, it must also be established that an expert opinion cannot be overridden by someone higher up the pyramid. The buck stops at expert level and nothing will sharpen judgement and responsibility more than this – nor increase status. Expertise must not, of course, encompass too large a field. Having settled first for a generic concept, it is of interest to read in the British Association of Social Workers' press release that encouragement may be necessary for 'specialization'. The child care field would appear to be a natural 'special field'.

INFORMATION

Correct information is essential for assessment. Right assessment leads to right actions. Assessment in a particular field is the function of the expert in that field. His skills must be developed to the point when he can make such assessments by himself. If information is not available, and he has reason to believe that others have it, he should seek that information himself. But it is not the function of other professionals to be able to divine his needs and supply information automatically. Confidentiality, which we will consider shortly, prevents a too easy handing out of information.

If assessment has failed, a common face saver is 'I was not told'. That is no excuse. An expert worker's own skills of assessment should give the answer without dependence on others. Taking a medical illustration we can see the value of this principle.

A patient is referred with attacks of breathlessness. The assessment of chest trouble is made. Later he is found to have a heart lesion. Years earlier the patient had been treated in another hospital for heart trouble. The clinician excuses his mistake with 'But they did not tell me that he had suffered from heart trouble before'. But this is no excuse, his examination should have been adequate enough to detect the heart trouble. Reports from others are merely complementary to adequate examination. Once every clinician relies on information from others, there will never be adequate examination. Similarly, assessment of families should not be dependent on past information from others, but on present careful and accurate assessment. Where will information come from, if no-one makes careful, accurate assessments? This is where expertise comes in.

Allied to flow of information is the matter of confidentiality, a greatly misunderstood matter. Information about a person belongs to that person, it is his goods. He conveys information from himself to another, his lawyer, for instance, only in as much as he has to lend the knowledge to be effectively helped. It is still his property and he does not wish it conveyed to others without his knowledge and consent, and even then only in order to be helped. If his trust is not respected, he has a simple answer: to convey nothing — or, if he does, he conveys what is irrelevant or useless. He can also elect not to seek help as this may be the lesser of two evils, when faced with the risk of loss of trust.

To respect confidentiality is of immense value to the helping professions and to the public. Every profession must have its ethical code. A computer centre, available to all the helping professions, because of lack of trust, could be full of useless information and the public would turn elsewhere for real help. There is — and rightly so — public unease about personal rights over confidentiality. An individual must know that when he addresses one person whom he trusts, he is not addressing the whole world. In the end families always frustrate those workers who do not have their trust.

Correct assessments of families is impossible unless there is absolute trust. For instance, Mrs. Kepple might have been glad to discuss Mr. Kepple and Maria. What held her back? Did she fear that the information might filter far and wide and ultimately destroy what was at that time for her an important relationship with her husband? But revelation in true confidence can bring the expert and the troubled wife together as a team to protect a child.

Sometimes there is a peculiar social class myopia over confidentiality. Families in lower income groups when in distress are expected to 'tell all'. The same would not be demanded of the bank manager, the chairman of the county council, or the director of education. Families resent this. There is something distasteful about professionals getting together in groups to discuss the intimate marriage, health and family problems of people without their presence, consent or knowledge. In psychiatry we meet problems of confidentiality daily — the chief constable and the tangle of his secretary, the priest and his masturbation problems, the headmistress and her broken lesbian love affair. Are these all matters for computer processing? People have ways of coping with loss of trust. The fantastic tales that they tell are astounding. Their tales not only obscure the truth, but are told with a deftness and artistry that almost compels admiration.

Records should be kept only with the individual's consent, and only for as long as they are required to help him. The information should then be destroyed. Far, far better, to maintain the community's trust and ensure a ready flow of information when it is required by paying the small price of re-obtaining the information. Incidentally, for research purposes, retrospectively obtained information is virtually valueless.

Confidentiality should be broken only in dire circumstances when the person concerned, or others, in calm judgement, would regard it as reasonable. The easier it is to break confidentiality the less people will work towards preserving it. There are many ways, short of breaking trust, of helping people. Neighbours may dislike reporting people for neglect of children. A little time getting to know the mother may soon give the mother what she wanted: a friend she could talk to − in trust. That discussion can lead to the mother accepting professional help. A trusting relationship makes it possible for her to convey all the information necessary to help her. Naturally, weight is given to positive evidence only. Not to know whether or not a foster father is adequate is not positive evidence of his suitability.

Children can often convey their views, if rightly approached, but one must be sensitive to a child's position. If he has known one home only and one lot of parents and is asked whether he would like to leave his home, he will invariably say 'no'. He will cling to what he knows, naturally. Only when he has been to more than one home can he make a judgement. A child often prefers to select between two 'goods' than a yes or a no. 'Is your mummy nice?' elicits 'yes'. But if asked 'Is your mummy nice or very nice?' then a 'Nice' indicates doubt, and yet he has been loyal.

In dire circumstances confidentiality may have to be broken. It is best done with the awareness of the person concerned, who later will often acknowledge the good sense of it. In dire circumstances it is not appreciated by the sufferer if we let him, in a drunken state or a diabetic coma, fall into a river.

SELECTION

Everyone who needs to use professionally a close interaction with another person should be selected for the capacity to make a warm relationship. This applies especially to staffs of day nurseries, nursery schools, schools, play groups, nannies, foster mothers, adoptive mothers and all the helping professions. It even applies to parents ultimately; when couples can admit their inability to give parenting, they may put aside a sense of duty to have children − or to seek to repair a marriage relationship by having a child, or to use an infant as an emotional lollipop.

Wise selection is particularly important in the helping professions. In these fields we suffer with a lack of knowledge about many aspects of human behaviour. Book learning is of little value compared with a balanced experience of life as it is. Thus one must rely on common sense, on experience — and the best experience comes from the best family background. Even wrong theory then will not be allowed to cloud judgement to the same extent. The heart will cry out against procedures that clash with fact and common sense. Unhappy deprived people often want to help deprived children because in them they see themselves. Theirs is a laudable objective, but the execution would be grossly hampered by the family experience that stands behind them.

Figure 10 — Two healthy and happy brothers

But how to select? From our earlier consideration of sick families, the principle emerges. An assessment must be made of childhood experiences. Sound, happy, warm families produce balanced warm people, able to relate to others. The examination of the past must be thorough. What may appear to be a bad home, may turn out to be a good one, e.g. a notorious unbalanced actress may be a child's mother, but the child was never brought up by her, but by an ideal nanny. Also, fortunately, restitution factors come along that may also help what are otherwise damaging situations.

Assessments of foster parents of course must be careful and prolonged. Foster parents, like natural parents, are mostly sound, some are indifferent, and some damaging. We have the opportunity to select the sound. The assessment turns around 'is there a capacity for loving care?' This is best estimated by assessing the fount of their capacity for loving

care — the preceding family. Other tests, of course, turn around relationships with others, success with their own children, low sickness
rate, good employment records, social involvement. Material circumstances have little to do with it. In the first textbook of paediatrics in
English, Thomas Phaire had this to say about the selection of a wet nurse:

... ye must be well aduised in takyng of a nource, not of ill com-
plexion and of worse maners: but suche as shalbe sobre, honeste and
chaste, well fourmed, amyable and chearefull, so that she may accus-
tome the infant vnto mirth, no dronkarde, vicious nor sluttysshe, for
suche currupteth the nature of the chylde.

It would be absurd and wrong to suggest that single people have less
capacity for loving care or relationships than the married. Nevertheless
to have been a wife and mother is an added advantage in the children's
field. To have experienced the throes of childbirth, the demands of
toddlers, the problems of schooling, the confrontation of adolescent
children, is valuable. Married people tend to be older. Age plus direct
experience with their own children inspire confidence in those to be
helped.

NON-COERCIVE ACTION

It follows from what has been said above that the immediate situation
of battered children is part of a larger situation, that of emotionally
deprived children. Organization should be aimed primarily at the main
situation, and then at the immediate situation of battered children. Policy
should be aimed at co-operative and non-coercive work with families,
with an emergency service able to rescue a child in dire straits.

The health professions must pay increasing attention to the matter
of emotional illness, with provision ranging from home level to specialist hospital services. Emotional illness is the responsibility of the health
professions and they cannot avoid it. Social services must steadily
deploy facilities to ameliorate emotional situations. It is their responsibility, and they cannot avoid it. The key to success is non-coercive
work with families by both services. Families approached in a helpful
way, especially with patience, will respond to approaches that ultimately lead to co-operation in solving their own adverse situations.
Even parents of battered children are usually aghast at the damage they
have done. Once the parents are approached in a way that will allow
them to express their anxieties, even in such an indirect way as saying
'we have so much that bothers us', it will be possible to offer them
help. Help carries supervision with it. When matters are beyond the

immediate family health workers and social workers, greater concentration of help and supervision is possible from the psychiatric services
specializing in emotional illness, preferably on a family basis. The
problem is never circumscribed to just a battered child; a battered child
is also a deprived child, the product of a depriving family, which needs
help in its own right.

In the case of a child requiring supervision, and with it the possibility of care elsewhere, it is clear that responsibility rests with the
social worker. We should not weaken this responsibility. The social
worker is able to initiate discussion with other useful agencies – health,
education, legal, etc. Usually, even parents of battered children have no
objection to being put in touch with a social worker when the child has
been reported to be at risk. In dire circumstances, when any reasonable
person would regard it as proper, a confidential warning by others, e.g.
school, police, hospital, general practitioner, health visitors, voluntary
societies, can be conveyed to the social work department. All children's
agencies must be alerted to the signs of a battered and deprived child.
There may be advantage in the social services department keeping a
confidential list of 'vulnerable families', as one might keep a list of
dangerously ill patients in a hospital.

In dire circumstances a child may need immediate removal to a place
of safety, a children's home, or, if requiring specialist care, a children's
psychiatric in-patient unit. A child admitted to hospital with injuries
which suggest that he has been battered, should always be referred to
the department of child psychiatry, which would automatically be in
touch with the social services department. A similar arrangement
already applies in the case of attempted suicide, where a patient is
always seen by a psychiatrist. In cases of doubt about returning the
child to his home, he should be retained in hospital until his safely can
be guaranteed. A battered child represents a depriving family and that
family too requires help.

MONOPOLY

The Monopolies and Restrictive Practices Act 1948 was established to
prevent monopolies against the public interest. Yet we have all but
created a monopoly in the care of our children, our most precious
asset, by vesting nearly all children's services in the state. Is this
wise? Voluntary societies are more flexible. They are an alternative and
a competitor.

Furthermore they are free to experiment. In large state organizations
creativity is at a minimum, unless there is specially instituted machinery. I am not talking of research, but innovation, creativity, new ideas.

Established opinions run state machines. To change such a machine is a daunting task. The more imaginative and worthwhile the idea, the greater the reaction of established opinion against it. Voluntary organizations can experiment, try pilot schemes, and, what is very important, lose money. Innovation must involve experimentation with uncertain results. To an auditor in a state machine to lose money is anathema. Those who carry responsibility tend to play safe.

There is a case, and a strong case, for the state to support an alternative to its monopoly in the care of children. Dr. Barnardo's and bodies like it should be encouraged to offer alternative residential services. The ever-open door should never be allowed to close. In the field, the NSPCC offers an alternative service. One might suppose that to be known as the 'cruelty man' might have aroused public antipathy, but remarkably the reverse applies — a tribute to a discreet, tactful, helpful service.

LEGAL RIGHTS

Mothers have rights, fathers have rights, children have rights. Just at the moment we tend perhaps to give too much weight to mother, despite her importance, when we come to judge who should have the custody of children. Father in certain circumstances is a better primary parenting figure. It is a matter of judgement, and both parents should be considered equally. Likelihood of marriage is a related factor, a borderline parent may be very adequate with a good partner, and that could apply to mother or father.

Foster parents too need protection from hasty removal of children; they need a right of appeal when this occurs, and independent legal help. Loving care of a child for three years should establish a case for adoption. If effectively loved for that period, a child can do no better elsewhere.

Wives have long ceased to be treated as chattels of the husband. But the child is hardly regarded as a citizen in his own right. He is often regarded as a property of his parents to be abused and misused as they please. Only in adolescence does he acquire the strength to protest. The adolescent's protest often hides the stifled cries of years. Maria Colwell was not seen by the court that sent her back to her parents. Perhaps, if the misconceptions can be buried, one opinion from a Social Service Department would be sufficient, especially if the law changes as recommended in the Houghton Report and the welfare of the child becomes paramount. If the court is in doubt it should seek a psychiatric opinion — someone acting as an independent expert on their behalf. But if the machinery is found not to work, if and when the law changes to give more protection to children, the public may be impatient for the appointment of an independent advocate to support the child. One of the difficulties is: where does the advocate get his opinions from? Such a person might still be insisting on the power of the 'blood tie'. It seems one can truly progress only at the pace of true knowledge. In many aspects we will have to wait on time. Knowledge depends on systematic investigation and that on money, men and resources.

Chapter 10

Afterthoughts

'Remember Maria' was the message printed on the placards which parents paraded outside the Court of Inquiry. The parents who held the placards were saying, 'Remember, a child died unnecessarily. Take the matter seriously. Keep in mind that whatever went wrong ended in the death of a child.' The very enormity of her death demands our attention. Her death occurred despite the fact that it was so obvious that she was being put at risk. Her death gives us the opportunity to re-examine our child care practices. It will be healthy to talk, but not for too long. Children at immediate risk cannot wait.

Behind the battered child is an army of deprived children. They are surging into the future to make more disturbed families with more Marias. Unhappiness feeds on unhappiness. The spiral of emotional deprivation must be halted. It can be halted.

Bibliography

Barker, R. G. and Wright, H. F. (1966). *One Boy's Day, a Specimen Record of Behaviour.* New York: Harper & Row.

Churchill, Randolph S. (1966). *Winston S. Churchill,* Vol. 1, *Youth.* London: Heinemann.

Churchill, Winston S. (1944). *My Early Life.* London: Macmillan.

Devore, I. (1963). 'Mother—infant relationships in three baboons.' In *Maternal Behaviour in Mammals,* Ed. by H. L. Rheingold. London/New York: John Wiley.

Mead, M. (1935). *Sex and Temperament in Three Primitive Societies.* London: Routledge and Kegan Paul.